Development
on a Human Scale

Peter van Dresser

Published in cooperation with
the Biotechnic Press

The Praeger Special Studies program—
utilizing the most modern and efficient book
production techniques and a selective
worldwide distribution network—makes
available to the academic, government, and
business communities significant, timely
research in U.S. and international economic, social, and political development.

Development on a Human Scale

Potentials for Ecologically Guided Growth in Northern New Mexico

PRAEGER SPECIAL STUDIES • DESIGN/ENVIRONMENTAL PLANNING SERIES

Praork   Washington   London

Library of Congress Cataloging in Publication Data

van Dresser, Peter.
    Development on a human scale.

    (Praeger special studies environmental/
design series)
    1. New Mexico—Economic conditions—Case
studies.   2. Regional planning—New Mexico—
Case studies.   3. Environmental policy—New
Mexico—Case studies.   I. Title.
HC107. N6V36   301. 31'09789'5   73-8179

PRAEGER PUBLISHERS
111 Fourth Avenue, New York, N.Y. 10003, U.S.A.
5, Cromwell Place, London SW7 2JL, England

Published in the United States of America in 1973
by Praeger Publishers, Inc.

Second Printing, 1973

Printed in the United States of America

Portions of the material used in this study were assembled by the author while
under contract to the New Mexico Office of Economic Opportunity, with Federal
funding. The concerned cooperation of the Office and their permission to publish
is gratefully acknowledged. Some other portions have appeared in the "New
Mexico Review," and their kind permission to reprint is also acknowledged.

FOREWORD

"There is much evidence," said zoologist Charles R. Goldman at the First Congress on Optimum Population and Environment, "that planning for a smaller future is in the best overall interest of mankind." A hard truth, perhaps, for a society that invented the skyscraper, the assembly line, bumper-to-bumper traffic, Superman, and consumership, but a truth all the same.

Bigness for bigness's sake lies close to the heart of American dogma. But where has bigness got us? The question is largely rhetorical, of course, because the answer can be *felt* by anyone who lets his senses and sensitivities register the impact of his everyday environment upon his consciousness. Bigness hurts. In legal parlance, bigness delivers torts — to the individual, to the community, to the political organism, and most grievously, to the human perspective. Bigness has produced the "crispies" culture.

We all know this, though we are loathe to probe very deeply into the substance of "the richest, most powerful nation on the face of the earth." We are afraid of what we might find. And yet, paradoxically, we might very well find the forgotten essence of what made the United States such a singular success in the first place.

I think we might find *ourselves* again. We might rediscover, for example, such blunted attributes as competence and personal gratification in work. We might realize the precariousness of the handhold on life itself maintained by an extractive technology and an extruded culture. Indeed, the American people, presented with an alternative, might begin to perceive the promise of a new — or shall we say old? — way of seeking the highest of all goals: self-fulfillment.

They might even swap their bowl of crispies for a nourishing sense of personal re-engagement in the shaping of their lives and their environment.

v

Toward this end, few students of the American experience have given more thought to the wisdom of Dr. Goldman's "smaller future" than Peter van Dresser. For more than twenty years, Mr. van Dresser has lived in the kind of micro-environment that might very well be transformed, carefully and unsensationally, into a model of social and ecological regeneration. Within the bioeconomic scope, and the immediate and intimate environs of the villages of the southern Rockies where he has made his home, there exists an exceptional opportunity to demonstrate the virtue of smallness.

This book will help us take the necessary first step towards activating this opportunity. This step must be, as the argument makes clear, the widespread recognition that many of the rural and provincial communities of the United States do, in fact, possess the resources to revitalize themselves; that revitalized micro-environments based, in Mr. van Dresser's words, on "skilled, scientific, and conservative use and management of local biotic and other flow resources, rather than on large-scale machine- and energy-intensive industries," can go a long way toward redressing the balance between industrial excesses and provincial impotence.

This is exciting stuff. From the standpoint of people needs and ecological responsibilities, Mr. van Dresser conceives of a biotechnic society in which both man and nature are well served. Research to be carried out in a micro-environment such as the uplands of northern New Mexico is urgently needed. And, in comparative terms, not very many dollars could be stretched a very long way to implement this hopeful idea. A growing number of Americans, including the young people who are groping for community through communes, are ready for the richness of human scale and scope. They are simply fed up with the depersonalizing effects of an extrusion society. I hope the promise of this author's thinking can be refined, implemented, and acted upon in the very near future. The country would be the better for it.

William Houseman
Editor, "The Environment Monthly"
June 24, 1970

TABLE OF CONTENTS

Table of Contents (continued)

INTRODUCTION

A few years ago speculative economists began discussing the approach of the "post-industrial age" — a coming era of affluence in which the chief business of man would be the distribution of automatically produced abundance, the elaboration of public amenities, and the enjoyment of leisure. Urbanists and city planners began projecting vertical, radial, domed, underground, floating, and ribbon cities to house the teeming millions to come. Engineers dreamed of agrochemurgic complexes, nuclear-generated energy fields, and automated transportation networks to serve the coming ecumenopolis.

In this vision, the growth or extraction of raw materials and their fashioning into commodities through mechanization and automation, was about to be raised to such a level of efficiency that only a small minority of men need henceforth devote their efforts to such activities. Correlatively, the distribution of commodities and services, the perfection of public amenities, and the creative use of leisure, would become the principal preoccupation of a society provisioned, housed, and serviced by an unfailing commissariat of "iron goblins" (to use Ruskin's anticipatory epithet for automated machinery).

Such a vision of post-industrial society supposed, of course, an indefinite extension and elaboration of the tremendous logistic apparatus which now ministers to our needs. It supposed a continued proliferation of the transportation, transit, and communications networks which serve an ever-expanding population either clustered in metropolitan areas or distributed in "non-place urban communities." It supposed ever more intricate factory complexes, deeper oil wells, huger wheat fields, vaster

ix

mining excavations, to supply the flow of energy and materials required by this enormous nexus of consumption.

The formidable statistical conclusions which the experts have been drawing from these suppositions are finally filtering into public consciousness. We are becoming aware of the astronomical quantities of coal and iron ore we will have to mine each year to keep the machinery going; of the floods of petroleum we must draw from ever deeper subterranean and subsea reserves; of the mountain ranges of garbage and wastes we must dispose of; of the major river basins we must reconstruct; of the oceanic and atmospheric circulation systems we must police; of the waxing hordes of megalopolitan and inter-urban dwellers we must house, feed, sanitate, and air condition.

The moderately long-term implications of these statistical trends boggle the mind. In a mere two or three centuries, the analysts see us crushing and digesting the very rocks of the earth's crust for their mineral content and for the traces of thorium and uranium they contain to power our atomic piles; the oceans' waters channeled through gigantic plants for the extraction of chemicals; the seven seas farmed for protein-yielding algae, and their deepest beds probed for nodules of meteoric minerals. They visualize colossal automated nuclear-powered agrochemurgic complexes pumping power, food, and synthetics into the all-embracing environmentally conditioned "ecumenopolis" or world city, in which mankind dwells.

It is not surprising that this vision of the not-so-distant future, even though it is shaped by the statistical projections of demographers, resource-economists, and planners, is arousing serious misgivings in many of us. The problems of global life-support system management which such an artificed world raises are utterly outside the limits of our knowledge. The question of the ultimate capacity of the human psyche to remain sane in an increasingly mechanical, controlled, and non-organic environment reaches into another unknown dimension.

Even today, when only a few nations are crossing the threshold of this brave new world, we are experiencing frightening dislocations of biospheric balance, environmental deterioration, and civil disorders. Well-nigh irresistible industrial and economic processes involving air, water, and land pollution, hydrologic cycle disruption, food chain poisoning, and the like, are rampant wherever giant technology, its works, or its waste products, interact with the landscape.

Popular reaction against the disturbing uncertainties of this looming future (which, in fact, began as long ago as the late 18th century) is expressing itself currently at high intensity in a literature of protest under the general banner of "ecology." Manifesto after manifesto have appeared denouncing the pollution-generating operations of the great metallurgical, chemical, automotive, agribusiness, and power corporations; control legislation has been debated in most state capitals and in Washington, and some of it has even been adopted; conservation candidates and parties have appeared; pickets and boycotts have been mounted; lists of austerities to be practiced by conscientious citizens have been drawn up and circulated.

Much of this agitation implies no basic questioning of the underlying premises of industrial society. Accepting as irrevocable the present trends in population growth and concentration, it takes for granted that the needs of the swarming generations to come must be met through a ceaseless refinement of the machine systems on which we have become dependent, and of the complex mass habitats in which we must dwell.

It assumes that the general apparatus of production and distribution will continue to function at even higher levels of output, efficiency, and complexity in the future, but that its harmful side effects will be eliminated by increasingly sophisticated technical and legal controls. Accordingly, this wing of the ecologic front calls for such ends as "action now" against belching smokestacks and spewing outfalls; for campaigns against waste and littering; for a halt to excessive scarifications and mutilations of the earth. It proposes, in short, to police the emerging landscape of megalopolis through intelligent planning, enlightened engineering, and responsible administration.

Such goals, commendable though they are, and realistic though they seem in the light of current conventional wisdom, are probably inadequate to the depth of the long-term ecologic crisis ahead. There are strongly argued opinions expressed in many quarters that even with the best of policing and decontamination measures, the web of life on earth can survive for no more than a few decades the continued expansion of our vast apparatus for planetary exploitation. A true reading of the ecologic "handwriting on the wall" confronting us, it is argued, unequivocally signals that our civilization must make a more profound adjustment to the vital processes of the biosphere than merely recycling our wastes, precipitating our effluents, banning persistent pesticides, and landscaping our freeways and borrow-pits.

It is very possible, despite such ameliorative efforts, that the sheer deadweight of urban aggregations, the insatiable materials-processing, transport and energy requirements built into our present pattern of economic organization will continue to intrude so insistently, so massively, and at so many points into the tissue of our living environment, that the damage may soon exceed the natural world's self-healing capability.

An obvious adjustment to this likelihood could be a slowdown in human multiplication, a stabilization of population, hopefully even an eventual reduction in absolute numbers in many parts of the world. This is a highly visible and widely discussed issue which could be described as the second major campaign front of the drive for ecologic reform. Although, as yet, distressingly little effect is visible in the growth-habits of most nations, an increasing number of organizations and public agencies are concerned with it, and much scientific research is devoted to the very difficult social, political, religious, and medical problems it poses.

A third and probably the least understood and explored aspect of the ecologic challenge is the strategy of adaptation through modifying our industrial system so as to drastically reduce both our per capita and total appetite for energy and for extracted, processed, fabricated, and transported things, while at the same time continuing to improve our level of civilization in terms of the more genuine material needs and cultural amenities.

The general outlines of this strategy have been sketched in by various explorers in such fields as urban, cultural, and political evolution, town and regional planning, human geography, speculative economics, and the like. The restructuring of our socioeconomic organization which could lead towards such results runs somewhat as follows:

1. There should occur a redistribution and regrouping of population, of means of production, and of patterns of trade in such a manner as facilitates greater local and regional self-sufficiency in the production of goods, services, and amenities.

2. As part of this regrouping, the smaller range of "urban places" (villages, towns, provincial cities) must undergo a renaissance as vital functional elements in the economic and cultural order, and this should be accompanied by corresponding diminishment in the relative importance of major cities and metropolitan conglomerations.

3. An increasing proportion of our over-all social effort should be diverted away from ubiquitous mechanized commutation and massive mechanized transport and distribution, and towards the enrichment and diversification of localized production within efficient smaller communities, as the enlightened solution of the "logistic" problem.

xii

4. A type of production technology should be encouraged which is adapted to the utilization of renewable "flow resources" (vegetative growth, climatic cycles and energies, etc.) on a small-scale, intensive, science-, skill-, and manpower-basis, rather than on a large-scale, extensive machine- and mechanical-energy-basis.

5. There should be a corresponding development of an ecologically grounded science of community design, adequate to guide the recolonization of vast semi-abandoned and under-used provinces of the nation on a sustained-yield, symbiotic basis with the soil, climatic, and biotic regimens of such regions.

6. Communication and education techniques should be developed such as will allow this organic type of population dispersion, renucleation, and regionalization to occur, while maintaining a high level of social and ecological awareness, and a degree of scientific and intellectual competence which will effectively counteract the dangers of parochialism and insularity.

It is clear that a social evolution of this general type can best occur in the "under-developed" and provincial areas of the nation, where cities and towns are still of manageable size, population densities are still low, and land and biotic resources are still relatively accessible and uncompromised. In such regions, our prime consideration should be to not repeat the dreary cycle of speculation, monopoly, over-centralization, and over-exploitation which is draining the economic and cultural vitality of our hinterlands and driving their populations into the slums, grey interurbs, and industrial wastelands of our overloaded metropolitan areas.

Here we can keep our communities, our villages, and our small cities in ecologic balance with the capabilities of the lands, forests, and waters surrounding them. We can substitute growth in intelligence, skill, and cultural completeness for growth in numbers, size, and dollar-measured GNP. We can ease the pressures of functionless production, consumption, and waste which are forcing us as a nation to mass pollution, mass violence, and global despoliation, and we can help set a viable pattern for the future.

Supposing such generalities as to a desirable future seem to make sense, how do we go about actualizing them? How and where do we start shifting the accumulated momentum of our social evolution?

This book attempts to answer such questions in terms of a specific regional community in the United States, which the author believes to exemplar both a classical pattern of rural-provincial decline and an unusual potential for regeneration. This regional community occupies a portion of the geographer's "southern Rocky Mountain province" of the West, about

xiii

the size of Switzerland. Here, by reason of a centuries-old adaptation to the land-forms and the vital resources, a special cultural heritage, and a relative isolation from the major urban-industrial zones of the continent, a life-style, land-use pattern, and local economy have maintained themselves which are especially amenable to concepts of "ecologic" growth and development.

It is nevertheless by no means certain that such development will occur. The complex mechanisms of modern civilization — governmental, commercial, financial — have been for generations at work throughout the region, and their accelerating effect may disastrously modify its fate within the next decade. Yet, because of the relative homogeneity and integration of this microcosm, it is possible to attempt an overall assessment of these factors. Hopefully we may then inventory policies which can facilitate a pattern of economic change harmonizing with ecologic principles. This pattern may, in turn, offer a model for the solution of our continent-wide problems of rural and provincial decline with all the environmental and social imbalances this entails.

Part One, following, presents a brief historical and geographical account of the growth of this regional community, of some of the reasons for the pattern of settlement and the lifestyle it embodies, and of various processes of private and governmental economic development and resources exploitation to which it has been subjected. The cumulative and generally negative effect in ecologic and environmental terms of these processes is discussed, and some lessons to be learned by viewing the situation in global perspective are pointed out.

Part Two focuses on a specific range of programs, projects, and institutional arrangements operating within the region, and comments on their socioeconomic effects as measured against ecologic criteria. Alternative and more desirable possibilities are outlined.

Part Three projects a pattern of regional growth and economic activity which might result from a consistent application of ecologically derived development principles over a quarter-century. The ability of the land and resources base to retain and support its present population — and, in fact, a considerably increased one — while maintaining a higher real standard of living and improving the condition of the soil, forests, and the general biotic community is discussed. The contribution this process could make to solving national and global problems of over-urbanization and environmental impoverishment is emphasized.

Part Four looks at the general nature of "natural resources" and attempts to clear up some misconceptions on this subject which affect the human use of the land in regions such as the uplands. The argument is presented that the basic resources of this region are ample to support a thriving and growing indigenous community, provided a life-style, technology, and land-use pattern appropriate to the environment continue to be nurtured. The difference in the conception of resources as viewed in this context from that dominated by conventional investment and export considerations is discussed. The wide applicability of the ecologically adapted and "bioeconomic" approach to development is again pointed out.

Part Five restates the general thesis in terms of the problem of urban regeneration which necessarily occupies the focus of much of our thinking in our increasingly urbanized society.

The rethinking and restructuring of our purposes, our institutions, and our private and public policies needed to effect such changes in the direction of our social and economic evolution on the scale that will be necessary is a colossal, dismaying, and fascinating task. As the final and most difficult phase of the ecologic transformation towards which all people are groping, its long-term consequences must, if we succeed, dwarf even those of the industrial revolution in permanence and ultimate meaning. May our vision sustain us over the difficult coming century.

Peter van Dresser
El Rito
Rio Arriba County
New Mexico
May 1972

PART ONE
THE SHAPING OF THE REGION

PART ONE

THE SHAPING OF THE REGION

Erosion and Physiography

Addressing a membership meeting of the newly formed Middle Rio Grande Conservancy District in Albuquerque in 1926, a keynote speaker, in his historical resumé, remarked that the problems of the region *"had been the subject of various reports and investigations for the past forty years!"**(Italics and exclamation point added.)

Since the nation was then at the height of the famous pre-depression boom of the '20s, collective sociological soul-searching was not in fashion and the emphasis of the talk was naturally not on social questions but on the financial, engineering, and hydrological problems pressing the District. These included river-bottom aggradation, periodic flooding, silt deposit, waterlogging and salting of soils, and the like.

So acute had these problems then become that, of a theoretical 128,000 acres of cultivatable land within the new District (which stretched from San Marcial in the south to White Rock Canyon in the north), a mere 60,000 was actually in use, and tax delinquency and farm bankruptcy were rife throughout the valley. The speaker did recognize that the underlying causes of many of these problems could be traced outside the official District boundaries to the abuses of soil and vegetation throughout the system of Rio Grande tributaries which drained the uplands of northern New Mexico and southern Colorado.

---

* **"The Middle Rio Grande Conservancy District,"** text of address at Conservancy Board meeting, September 1926.

In considerably less than a decade, the cautious note of warning sounded in this address was reverberating heavily throughout New Mexico and, in fact, throughout the nation. The financial crash of 1929 had touched off the Great Depression and it became obvious that the physical erosion which was worrying the Conservancy District engineers in the 1920s was a mere symptom of economic, cultural, and human erosion which had been going on for some time throughout the province of mountain-based villages upstream from Albuquerque.

In physical terms, this province consists of the southward extension, across the 37th parallel, of that massive spinal ridge of North America which we call the Rocky Mountains (Fig. 1). An island or peninsula of wooded and forested uplands country rising above the general semi-desert of sagebrush and drought-resistant grasses, results from this intrusion, rarely sinking as low as 6,000 feet above sea level and touching 13,000 feet in its highest rises. The storied Rio Grande bisects this island into two major eastern and western ranges — the Sangre de Cristo and the San Juan — and, gathering sustenance from a sequence of swift and steep streams fed from the snows and rains of the higher courses, plunges on southward and eventually eastward toward Texas, Mexico, and the Gulf.

The upthrust of this great land-mass into the higher, cooler atmosphere creates naturally a climatic zone markedly different from that of most of New Mexico. So pronounced is that demarcation that the Weather Bureau designates a "Northern Mountain Sector," in the State's climatic map. Within this sector, especially in the upper two-thirds of its land-mass, one encounters true winter seasons with night temperatures often in the neighborhood of zero, and with long-lasting snow packs. The annual precipitation averages probably 20 inches and rises over 30 at the highest points — as contrasted with an average of perhaps 10 inches for the Lower Rio Grande Basin.

But perhaps the most significant expressions of climate here are the year-round curves of atmospheric water balance (Fig. 2) which show an average precipitation deficiency of only 9 to 10 inches for this region, as contrasted with the average of 22 for the lowland bulk of the State. This accounts for the much higher vegetation density within the region in spite of the relatively short growing season for commercial crops (79 to 178 days).

This climatic environment, in turn, brings into being distinctive flora and animal life. Bailey, the great naturalist, identified five life-zones in New Mexico well over a generation ago. Three of these — the "Upper Sonoran," the "Transition," and the "Canadian" — make up the great bulk of the

4

Figure 1

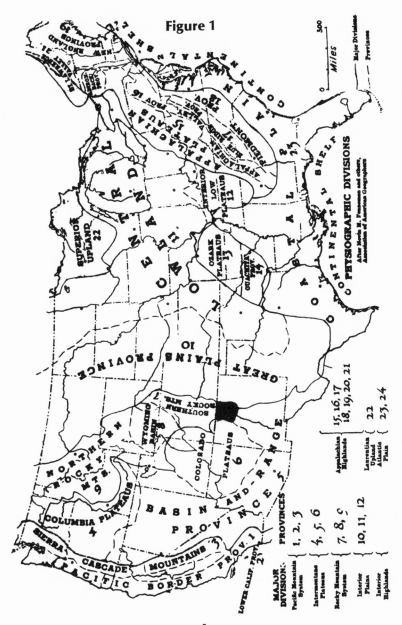

PHYSIOGRAPHIC DIVISIONS

After Nevin M. Fenneman and others,
Association of American Geographers

MAJOR	DIVISION:	PROVINCES:
Pacific Mountain System	{	1, 2, 3
Intermontane Plateaus	{	4, 5, 6
Rocky Mountain System	{	7, 8, 9
Interior Plains	{	10, 11, 12
Interior Highlands	{	13, 14
Appalachian Highlands	{	15, 16, 17, 18, 19, 20, 21
Laurentian Upland	{	22
Atlantic Plain	{	23, 24

5

Figure 2

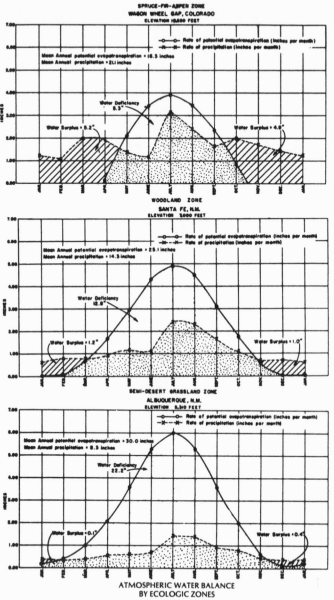

ATMOSPHERIC WATER BALANCE
BY ECOLOGIC ZONES

6

living world of this region, as the accompanying map shows (Fig. 3). The upper two are characteristically the zones of the great coniferous forests which Bailey spoke of as "natural parks." Some 137 species of animals and 70 of trees and shrubs have been identified within these zones, ranging from the great elk through mule deer and brown bear to the tiniest shrew and hummingbird; from the massive ponderosa to the golden-blossoming rabbit brush, locally called "chamisa." The lowest of these three zones, the Upper Sonoran, still classifies as "woodland," but its tree cover is mostly the sparser juniper and pinon pine, and the soil is often steep and highly erodable.

The same characteristic is repeated on a map of the commercial forests of northcentral New Mexico prepared by the State Economic Development Commission (Fig. 4). On the basis of these and other criteria, one can outline a quite specific region which we may call New Mexico's Northern Uplands Province and which, upon closer study, reveals many distinctive cultural and physical characteristics.

In topographic terms, this region or province is one of high relief; it is broken horizontally by upheaved mountain masses and the characteristic mesa forms resulting from the erosion of ancient sea bottoms; it is dissected vertically by the canyons and steep valleys of the numerous streams which traverse it. These streams are mainly tributaries of three major basins — the Rio Grande, the Pecos, and the Canadian — and, in fact, supply a large fraction of the stable flows of these important rivers. The entire region may thus be considered as "headwaters country" — a fact whose significance will be discussed later.

History of Settlement

Although the remnants of the early Spanish northernmost colonizations in the new world are scattered throughout New Mexico (and, indeed, the entire Southwest), this north-central portion of the State is the area *par excellence* in which this cultural heritage in the first decades of this century fully dominated the landscape. Over an area of some 13,000 square miles, a somewhat archaic and provincial Spanish was the prevailing tongue. Adobe villages clustered about the protecting church were the characteristic form of settlement. Community *acequias* or irrigation ditches watered the fields

7

Figure 3

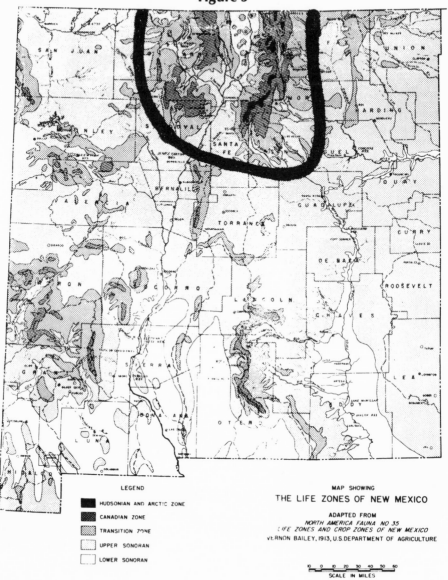

LEGEND

- ■ HUDSONIAN AND ARCTIC ZONE
- ▨ CANADIAN ZONE
- ▦ TRANSITION ZONE
- □ UPPER SONORAN
- □ LOWER SONORAN

MAP SHOWING
THE LIFE ZONES OF NEW MEXICO

ADAPTED FROM
NORTH AMERICA FAUNA NO 35
LIFE ZONES AND CROP ZONES OF NEW MEXICO
VERNON BAILEY, 1913, U.S.DEPARTMENT OF AGRICULTURE

SCALE IN MILES

Figure 4

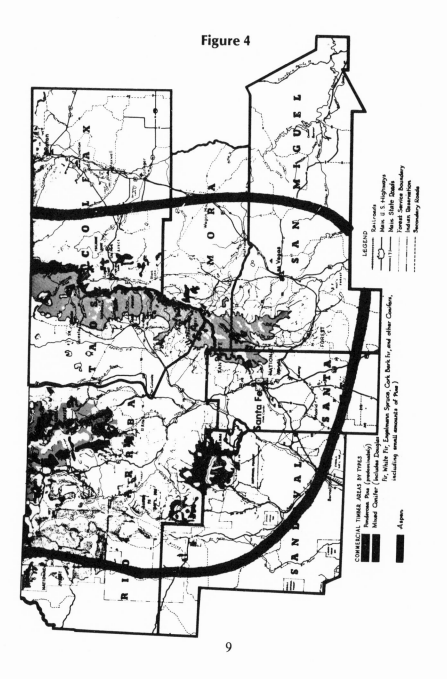

under the direction of *mayordomos*. The local large landholder or merchant played the economic and social role of the *patron* of earlier centuries to the majority of his neighbors; and these neighbors celebrated the Saint's Day of their village with procession, *fiesta,* and old-worldy ritual.

This former Spanish colonial province had been, in fact, for centuries the only area of relatively stable and intensive European settlement in the interior of the North American far west. Of necessity, it had been a province of primarily subsistence-oriented mountain and foothill villages, clustered in the valleys of the southern Rockies. Here the rigors of the semi-desert Southwest were tempered by altitude, and the tributaries of the Rio Grande, upper Pecos, and Canadian rivers could be diverted by simple hydraulic works to irrigate small farms capable of providing the basic necessaries of life.

These settlements — which, incidentally, stretched over a region almost as large as Switzerland — were for generations sustained by a simple but effective subsistence and pastoral agriculture, had evolved an architecture and a handicraft technology well adapted to the land, and were enriched by folkways and ecclesiastic institutions of considerable stability and dignity. Santa Fé, the tiny capital of this mountain province, had a provincially old-world and Latin character quite unlike any other North American city. The region for which it served as metropolis, although technically a part of the United States since the Treaty of Guadalupe-Hidalgo, was virtually a foreign country whose way of life, however strange and archaic it may have seemed to eastern visitors, had an undeniable vitality and self-sufficiency.

As late as 1910, the inhabitants of this provincial region constituted a good 30% of the population of New Mexico, even though, geographically, it represented only 10% of the State's total land area (Table 1).

Table 1
Population, Northcentral New Mexico* vs. New Mexico, 1910-1970
(in thousands, rounded to nearest hundred)

	1910	1920	1930	1940	1950	1960	1970(est.)
NNM	98.4	105.0	113.0	144.8	155.8	156.6	190.0
NM	328.0	360.4	423.3	531.8	681.2	951.0	1220.0
%	30	29	27	27	22	16	16

(Adapted from Table 5, "Projections of the Population of New Mexico and Its Counties," New Mexico Business, July and August, 1965.)

* Colfax, Mora, Rio Arriba, Sandoval, San Miguel, Santa Fé, Taos, and Los Alamos Counties.

10

By the opening years of the 1930s, however, this former Spanish Crown Colony, Mexican Province, and United States Territory had been for almost a generation a full-fledged member of the great North American union, and circumstances were changing drastically. While the old "Rio Arriba" province still contained 27% of the State population, a new-era influx of Anglo-American or "Anglo" ranchers, homesteaders, and entrepreneurs had filled in many of the blank areas around it. New urban centers had sprung up at strategic locations on the transcontinental and regional railways and highways, and a new style of livelihood and land use had come into existence in New Mexico, as throughout the rest of the West, based on cheap government land, the eastern livestock market, railroad and motor transport, bank credit, barbed wire, wind pumps, and the deep-drilled well.

This overpowering wave of 20th century progress inevitably disrupted life in this traditional enclave. The sparse Spanish settlements farther south along the Rio Grande had begun to feel the impact of such changes early in territorial days but, as the new century progressed, they began to penetrate the traditionally self-contained highlands of the southern Rockies. Here subsistence farming, sheepherding, and village trades began to yield before the sophisticated goods and the higher incomes, costs, and taxes of this new style of life. The economic disparity was aggravated by loss to the newcomers of grazing and forest lands from the old grants and commons even within this mountain stronghold, through financial leverage often enough backed up with legal chicanery and fraud. Younger people of the uplands villages began that outbound trek in search of city jobs from California to Michigan which has continued ever since. Along with this export of talent, there also began a reluctant abandonment of beloved villages and farmsteads, an attrition of long-established customs and skills, and a disappearance of the tradition-laden way of life.

At the same time, the attempt to participate in the new commercial economy through massive livestock grazing and export, carried on both by the immigrating Anglo ranchers and such of the old *hacendados* and *encomienderos* as could maintain a grip on the necessary financial and land resources, was responsible for accelerating the soil and grass destruction resulting in much of the plague of erosion, arroyo-cutting, and flooding which harassed the Middle Rio Grande Conservancy District administrators. From the primarily subsistence grazing of relatively small herds and flocks in the neighborhood of settlements, characteristic of colonial and provincial days, the number of sheep herded in the Middle Valley leaped from 435,000 in 1870 to 1,732,000 in 1900, while cattle grew

11

from 14,000 to 211,000 in the same period.* For the State as a whole, the cattle census reached an all-time high of 1,095,000 in 1910, and the corresponding sheep count climbed to 3,759,000.**

Thus the former heart of the old Hispanic Southwest, while its four-footed population was increasing at a prodigious rate, was ironically losing its human population and was on its way to becoming the "land of forgotten people," to use George Sanchez' oft-quoted phrase. During the decade 1930-1940, the region's proportion of State population dropped to less than one-fourth and this decline was to continue over the next three decades. At the same time, such statistical indicators of relative socioeconomic wellbeing as are available (income level, years of education, percentage of productive-age citizens, housing quality index) consistently showed lower percentages than corresponding indices for New Mexico as a whole, and for the United States as a whole. (See Table 2.)

The Era of Public Programs

The era of quiet and unpublicized deterioration, however, came to an end early in the Great Depression which, in New Mexico, was complicated by the severe droughts of the 1930s and by the presence of thousands of unemployed and relatively articulate veterans of the first world war. At this time, the national government, suddenly aware of alarmingly spreading areas of poverty and unemployment within its borders, marshalled the "New Deal" generation of sociologists, economists, and resource planners against this threat, with a mandate to draft remedial programs of unprecedented boldness and scope. As part of this nationwide effort, the National Resources Planning Board undertook a monumental study of the Upper Rio Grande Basin, and an Inter-Departmental Rio Grande Board was formed in 1937 by Secretaries Wallace and Ickes of the Departments of Agriculture and the Interior. The hope behind this move seems to have been that a scheme as

---

* **"Man and Resources of the Middle Rio Grande Valley,"** University of New Mexico Press, 1943.
** **"An Economic Analysis of New Mexico History,"** Bureau of Business Research, University of New Mexico, 1967.

Table 2
AGE AND SEX OF POPULATION
U.S., and Rural Households of North Central New Mexico, 1957

AGE GROUP *

MALE   FEMALE

70-74
60-64
50-54   U. S.
40-44
30-34
20-24   New Mexico
10-14
0-4

% 9   6   3   0   3   6   9

*75 YEARS OR MORE

U.S. DEPARTMENT OF AGRICULTURE   *AGRICULTURAL RESEARCH SERVICE*

From "Rural People and Their Resources,
North-Central New Mexico"
NMSU, 1960

* * * * * *

Indices of Level of Living, North-Central New Mexico

	% Unemployed			% Families Having 1959 Incomes-			% 1960 Pop. Completing School Yrs.		1960 Housing Quality	
	1950	1960	1965	Under 2000	5000-7000	7M-10M	12	16	Sewer Conn.	H&C Wtr
NCNM RDA*	7.3	12.3	13.4	52.2	13.3	8.2	28.5	12.3	24.6	44.4
N. Mexico	2.5	5.5	5.5	20.9	19.0	15.5	43.1	20.6	42.8	82.0
U.S.A.	5.3	5.6	4.6	21.4	23.0	20.1	43.8	16.5	N/A	87.3

*North-Central New Mexico Redevelopment Area

Adapted from Tables 11, 13 & 14, **"Over-All Economic Development Program, Phase 1"**
NCNM Economic Development District, 1968.

13

comprehensive and ambitious as the Tennessee Valley Authority operation, which was then under way in a similarly stricken mountain river basin of the Appalachians, might be brought into reality here.

From this period to the present day "Northern New Mexico" and its ecologic, social, and economic problems have been the subject of a more or less continuous sequence of studies, analyses, programs, and projects originated by successive generations of agencies and institutions.

The complex of New Deal efforts, beginning in the early 1930s, launched this campaign with a vigor and all-embracing ambition probably not since equalled. This first period of governmental socioeconomic improvement efforts was strongly oriented towards land reform, conservation, and folk or family agriculture. Agencies such as the Emergency Relief Administration, the Resettlement Administration, the Grazing Service (later the Bureau of Land Management) purchased over 6 million acres of land in the middle and upper Rio Grande basin and consolidated numerous small grants and holdings for controlled use by Indian pueblos or Spanish communities. The Forest Service and Soil Erosion Service (reorganized later as the Soil Conservation Service) either through collaborative contract with private land owners or through intensified regulation of public lands, sharply cut back grazing on several million more acres.

Other lands were reclaimed for local users associations through low-interest loans provided by the Farm Security Administration. A king-sized "Rio Grande District" embracing most of the middle and upper Rio Grande basin, operating through 27 sub-projects covering over one and one-half million acres of land, carried out extensive and varied erosion control, revegetation, and reforestation works. In 1936, 4,200 CCC workers (Civilian Conservation Corps) in some 33 camps were supplying most of the manpower for this basic land-restorative effort.*

The Inter-Departmental Rio Grande Board in the latter years of this period were pushing ahead with still more advanced planning in collaboration with numerous State and Federal agencies involving human resources and cultural surveys, community development programs, health, special education, and vocational training proposals, public works coordination, and the like.

The approach of World War II, however, brought most of this activity to a halt. The Board suspended its activities early in 1942, and the attraction

* **"Annual Report, Rio Grande District, Soil Conservation Service,"** June 30, 1936.

14

of high-paying defense jobs on the Coast siphoned away thousands of unemployed from New Mexico and temporarily relieved the chronic "depressed area" status of the northern uplands. Very shortly after the war's close, however, the persistent land deterioration tendencies of the region were again demanding attention. In 1947, the Bureau of Reclamation and the Corps of Engineers published thick reports on the flood-control problem of the upper Rio Grande.* Four years later, a multi-agency Department of Agriculture study of runoff and waterflow retardation and soil-erosion prevention in the Rio Grande watershed was drafted.** This called for a $58 million outlay on a variety of conservation, water, and soil management and landscape improvement practices over most of the middle and upper basin. The benefit-cost ratio of this program was estimated at 3.08 to 1, over a 100-year amortization period. The spectrum of social and economic services contemplated in the pre-war programs was, however, not included in these immediate post-war proposals.

These other aspects of the northern New Mexico uplands situation did not remain permanently neglected. Perhaps aided by the global spotlight on "have-not" and "underdeveloped" peoples which the worldwide unrest following the close of the war was bringing into ever-sharper focus, a second generation of major government strategisms against "rural poverty" came into existence during the 1950s. Probably the earliest of these was the "RAD" (Rural Areas Development) program of the Department of Agriculture which, during the latter 1950s and early 1960s, maintained special staff workers in northern New Mexico organizing a network of improvement and development committees. This program, in turn, was supplemented by President Kennedy's "ARA" (Area Redevelopment Administration), which continued similar work but with somewhat broader powers. This newer organization stressed the idea of the "OEDP" (Over-All Economic Development Plan) to be prepared by local committees, usually

---

*   **"Rio Grande Tributaries, New Mexico,"** Survey for Flood Control, U.S. Army Corps of Engineers, 1947, 68 p.; and **"Plan for Development, Middle Rio Grande Project,"** U.S. Bureau of Reclamation, 1947, 213 p.

**   **"Survey Report (Interim), Rio Grande Watershed,"** U.S. Department of Agriculture, December 1951.

15

representing counties, and intended to guide and coordinate all economic development projects within each area of authorization.

The ARA was closely followed, after President Kennedy's assassination, by President Johnson's two-pronged campaign embodied in the "EOA" (Economic Opportunity Act) and the "EDA" (Economic Development Act). By the latter 1960s, the enabling power embodied in these acts had resulted in the establishment of a nine-county "North Central New Mexico Development District," whose boundaries embraced the uplands region, with some margin to spare. Additionally, there were a phalanx of "CAP" (Community Action Programs) covering the counties and Indian pueblos of the region, and later a "CEP" (Concentrated Employment Program) authority also centered on the uplands, but with some overlap into depressed counties elsewhere in the State.

These regionwide EDA and "OEO" (Office of Economic Opportunity) programs were supplemented by the Northern Rio Grande "RC&D" (Resources Conservation and Development) District, operating under Department of Agriculture sponsorship. This District was formed by local citizens in 1964 to work with the long-term Department policy of regional economic improvement centered around conservation and soil restoration activities. The authorized area for this program was, significantly, defined in terms of the Upper Rio Grande drainage — a continuation of long-standing basin-management concepts. Like the rest of the constellation of county-, pueblo-, or region-wide programs, this was steered by an elective board of commissioners, employing technical staff paid mostly out of Federal funds.

Three major engineering projects in the field of riverflow management also were completed or launched in the uplands region during this period. The earliest (1935), El Vado Dam on the Chama River, stores and regulates water for the Middle Rio Grande Conservancy District. Abiquiu Dam and Reservoir, downstream from El Vado, is a $40 million Corps of Engineers project, built in 1963, intended for desilting and flood control, with eventual recreational possibilities. The San Juan-Chama diversion project, still under construction, is a system of dams, tunnels, and canals intended to divert San Juan River water into the upper Rio Grande. This $70 million project will make available additional water for irrigated lands in the uplands region, although about two-thirds of its output will be absorbed in the Albuquerque and Middle Rio Grande Conservancy District area.

16

Besides these large projects and programs in the uplands, there has been a more or less continuous succession of smaller-scaled efforts, amongst which may be mentioned the Taos County Project and the Nambe Community School, financed by private foundations, and the Church and Community Cooperation Program of the United Presbyterian Board of Missions. Currently the "HELP" (Home Education and Livelihood Program) is the most ambitious of this tradition of religious and eleemosynary-inspired programs, sponsored as it is by the New Mexico Council of Churches (although, to a considerable extent, financed by Federal migratory labor funds). Although not focused exclusively on the uplands region, the majority of its community training centers, craft and small industry projects, are located there. VISTA, Peace Corps, and State Youth Corps volunteers have also worked more or less continuously throughout the region since the inception of these organizations, either on independent local projects or as staff aides in regular agency or anti-poverty activities.

There should also be mentioned in this context of subsidized economic development aids to the region the five REA cooperatives operating there which, since the enabling legislation was set up in the 1930s, have brought central-plant electric power to most of the settlements of any size in the uplands and to various industrial plants.

Finally, it should be recognized that the regular operations of many agencies — both State and Federal — often merge into this class of special public programs for economic and social improvement. Amongst these agencies should be mentioned the State Departments of Education and of Health and Welfare (now Health and Social Services); the State Library Commission, State Engineer Office, Department of Game and Fish, Parks Commission, and Forest Service; the Extension and Soil Conservation Services, the U.S. Forest Service, the Bureau of Land Management, Bureau of Reclamation, Army Corps of Engineers, and others. It would require a substantial research effort to even properly compile a list of such operations. Since they are usually set up on a State or nationwide basis and are not specific to northern New Mexico, it must suffice to simply mention them here.

17

Recent Key Reports on the Region

No complete bibliography of the special surveys, reports, work programs, and manuals generated by this spectrum of socioeconomic improvement activities in the region has so far been compiled. In its absence, brief resumés of a few major documents which have appeared in the last dozen years will serve to place the subject in recent historical perspective and point the general direction of technical, professional, and "official" opinion on the status of man, his works, and his environment in this regional community.

Watershed Resources and Problems of the Upper Rio Grande, U.S. Forest Service, Forest and Range Experiment Program, September 1956.

This is a 107-page carefully documented study published by the Rocky Mountain Forest and Range Experiment Station on the land-use, vegetation, landscape deterioration, flood control, and water-supply problems of the Rio Grande basin from Elephant Butte Dam to its headwaters in Colorado. This report inventories and discusses past and projected hydraulic engineering works in the basin, which then totaled nearly $600 million in cost. It concludes that this massive investment in control works "falls far short of controlling sediment inflow into the valley," and recommends that they be backed up by extensive erosion, sediment control, and revegetation programs on the land itself if the region's economic prosperity is to be restored and its expected population growth sustained.

The Timber Resources of Northern New Mexico, New Mexico Economic Development Commission, 1958.

This 55-page study represents a pre-"War on Poverty" attempt by a non-Federal agency to appraise the forest resources of the northern uplands as a basis for economic development of the region. The author tentatively

18

estimates the sustained yield annual output of the 3,000 square miles of commercial timber land at 121 million board feet. He recommends harvesting by selective thinning and more intensive conservation and silviculture practices which could probably increase the annual output over time. Waste in the field and at the mills is discussed as well as forest products other than timber. Possible industries utilizing this material are listed. No overall employment magnitudes or economic benefits are estimated, although some statistics are given on wood-using industries in the State and on the in-State market for paper and paperboard. The lack of accurate information on a number of phases of forest management and productivity is pointed out.

The San Juan-Chama Project, House Document 424, U.S. Bureau of Reclamation, June 1960.

This 461-page publication of the Department of the Interior is primarily an engineering and accounting analysis of the costs, revenues, and economic benefits of the long-discussed diversion of unappropriated San Juan River waters into the upper Rio Grande basin. The introductory section of this proposal lays considerable stress on the "critical conditions in the tributary units, long recognized as northern New Mexico's most pressing problem. . . . All counties in which the proposed tributary units are located have been classified by the State Economic Security Commission as labor depressed areas as a result of the high unemployment."

This project calls for an "initial phase" diversion of some 110,000 acre-feet of water annually into the Chama River by means of hydraulic works (dams, tunnels, canals) costing about $70 million. Of this supply, about 58,000 acre-feet were earmarked for municipal and industrial use (mostly in the vicinity of Albuquerque), 23,000 acre-feet were assigned for supplementary irrigation in the Middle Rio Grande Conservancy District, and 30,000 to irrigation of about 28,000 acres of farmlands in four uplands valleys of northern New Mexico. This last use was contingent upon the formation of local districts with taxing power capable of assuming responsibility for maintenance and partial repayment on local structures costing an additional $35 million. The benefit-cost ratio for this portion of

19

the project, if carried out, was estimated at 1.05:1. The general project was subsequently authorized by the 87th Congress and work was begun on the diversion tunnels and main dam in 1963.

Rural People and Their Resources, North-Central New Mexico, New Mexico State University, Agricultural Experiment Station and the U.S. Department of Agriculture's Agricultural Research Service, October 1960.

This 28-page illustrated statistical report was compiled to "provide information that might be useful in programs designed to alleviate the . . . economic, social, and cultural barriers and obstacles that have fostered and perpetuated a serious low-income problem . . . in the rural areas in the upper Rio Grande Valley." Much of the information presented was secured by direct interview with sample families and consists of data on household characteristics, farm characteristics, levels and sources of income, and availability for employment. The authors' appraisal lays emphasis on low cash income, subliteracy, lack of industrial skills, small size of farm units, and inefficient agricultural practices.

Development Potentials of the Northern New Mexico Uplands, prepared for the Regional Development Association of Northern New Mexico by Peter van Dresser, 1962.

This 40-page study, with appendix and tables, represents the earliest attempt to evaluate the uplands region as a physiocultural whole, with some consideration of the inter-relation between settlement and livelihood patterns, and the land and natural resources base. The argument is presented for an economic development process based on the historical valley-village. The "microbasin" is suggested as a feasible unit of development research, planning, and organization in the non-urban portion of the region, and estimates are presented for employment and productivity resulting from the scientific management of land and water on a skill- and manpower-intensive basis within such units. These estimates suggest that such use of the indigenous resources could support a considerably increased population at a higher standard of living.

Work Plan, Northern Rio Grande Resources Conservation and Development District, U.S. Soil Conservation Service, 1964.

This 85-page document is primarily an inventory of specific needs and potential projects within the boundaries of the District incorporated under the enabling powers of Public Law 87-703. Amongst such projects are improvements on about 200 local *acequia* systems, totaling $2.7 million by 1980, installation of domestic water and/or sewer systems in 19 communities, six small reservoir proposals at an estimated cost of $3.4 million, and several watershed protection proposals. Further, longer-ranged activities are also examined including various industrial and agricultural processing operations, recreational facilities, marketing co-ops, and mining developments.

Recent Demographic Changes in Northern New Mexico and **One Approach to the Economic and Social Problems of Northern New Mexico,** University of New Mexico, Bureau of Business Research, September 1964.

An economist and a sociologist of somewhat different schools of thought apply the analytic tools of their respective disciplines to the human situation in northern New Mexico. Statistics are presented documenting the lagging status of the regional population in such terms as income, literacy, and health, the outmigration of productive-age citizens, the disadvantagement of Spanish-surname employed, and the decline in agricultural income. The economist argues against "romantic" notions of the "soul-wearying poverty" he concludes to be characteristic of the region and against the viability of the village type of economy. He urges that "policy-making individuals . . . examine the facts straight on . . . to set about with expert guidance to plan and execute programs which will benefit the area most."

The sociologist discusses cultural conflict, historical economic phases,

21

and the reasons for failure of area programs. He recommends a comprehensive economic improvement program guided by a regional council and implemented through intensive agricultural training, small-scaled skilled industrial development, and the fuller utilization of forest resources and products, including recreation.

Both agree that northern New Mexico must be given vigorous assistance if it is not to remain a drag on the rest of the State.

Over-All Economic Development Program, Phase 1, North-Central New Mexico Economic Development District, May 1968.

This 286-page compendium was produced in compliance with EOA legislation requiring the preparation of a plan by each authorized Economic Development District. Information on the eight counties officially composing the District is presented under 15 categories, viz: Geography, Physical Description, and Climate; Land Ownership; Justification of Designation; Economic History; Population Characteristics; Minority Groups; Indians; Economy; Financial Capacity; Natural Resources; Transportation and Community Facilities; Growth Centers; Tentative Conclusions; and Current Efforts.

The material presented is mostly a compilation from standard statistical and administrative sources. Some analysis of present and potential "growth centers" in the region is attempted, in accordance with OEO prescriptions, and it is concluded that Santa Fé ranks first in desirability in this function, with Los Alamos, Raton, Espanola, Las Vegas, Taos, and Bernalillo following, in the order of listing. The section on "Justification" reiterates long-standing generalizations on the "poverty-stricken" character of the region, as indicated by educational deficiencies, past exploitation, inefficient traditional land division, social disintegration, etc. "Tentative Conclusions" are mostly of the same derivative nature and, amongst the causes of "Problems and Deficiencies" are listed outmigration of the enterprising citizens, inadequate education and training, limited labor markets, inaccessibility of raw materials, poor housing, lack of capital, inadequate roads, unmerchantable land titles, insufficient rail transport.

Water and Related Land Resources, Chama-Otowi Sub-Basin, Upper Rio Grande Basin, U.S. Department of Agriculture and State

Engineer of New Mexico, 1968 (Preliminary).

While this report does not deal with the "uplands" region as a whole, the sub-basin studied represents a large portion of that region, and companion studies covering the Red River-Embudo, and the Jemez-San Felipe sub-basins will substantially encompass most of northcentral New Mexico viewed as a physiographic unit rather than as a grouping of political jurisdictions (counties).

This document may be considered as the most recent and sophisticated of the Agriculture Department's application of the river basin type of analysis to New Mexico's economic problems and potentials. Starting with an overview of the sub-basin as a mosaic of land types, land uses, vegetative areas, and water- and sediment-yielding areas, the report evaluates conservation, soil, water, and vegetative management needs for each element of the mosaic; estimates manpower and monetary requirements for such practices; and calculates resulting annual dollar benefits in five categories (Increased Water Yield, Increased Timber Yield, Reduction in Sediment, Increased Production from Cultivated Land, and Increased Meat Production). These benefits are computed in excess of $6 million annually for a 15-year "early action" program of this type. Accompanying increase in annual income within the sub-basin is estimated at $345,209.

In addition to the "early action" (15 years) program, the report evaluates longer-term possibilities as well as those pertaining to the work of other agencies. These include potential for developing an additional 200,000 acres of irrigated lands in the sub-basin over the present 43,000 by improved and revised water-management practices, expanded recreational facilities, intensified silviculture and forest products utilization, etc.

Will the Future Repeat the Past?

The burden of most of this recent sequence of commentaries on the human condition in the Hispanic Rockies is surprisingly similar to what we read in the corresponding literature of one and two generations past. The same physical problems present themselves — for decade after decade — soil erosion, river silting, floods, declining agricultural production. Ambitious

23

public programs are outlined calling for vastly stepped-up engineering and conservation works. The statistics remain stubborn, always indicating a reluctance of the regional community to participate wholeheartedly in the general march of industrial and commercial progress. The "productive age" inhabitants continue to "outmigrate"; per capita possession or enjoyment of the various perquisites of modern civilization continue to lag behind national standards. "Job-creating industries" continue to bypass the region in their endless quest for "labor pools," "mass markets," and "accessible raw materials."

The cold comfort proffered in a 1967 "Economic Analysis of New Mexico History" by the State Bureau of Business Research, University of New Mexico, seems to apply with particular force to the northern uplands:

> The critical importance of economic development to our State is not so much that it will allow us to catch up with the national average level of living, as it is that it will keep us from falling farther and farther behind. Just keeping pace with the upward-moving national average level of living will be a demanding exercise.

Is the future of this unique region, then, culturally rich and in many respects well endowed by nature to be shaped simply by a continuation of the dominant trends of the past half-century? Will the studies and reports written a generation from now still speak of "chronic rural depression," "disadvantaged minorities," "lagging economy," "aging and out-migration of population," as they have for so many decades? Or are new forces at work in our society capable of carrying this regional community into a brighter and more vigorous realization of its potentials?

In attempting to answer such questions, it is at this point useful — in fact, essential — to view the whole question in the context of certain pervasive long-term influences that must be taken into consideration if we hope to evaluate realistically future courses of evolution and action.

Metropolitanization — A Dominant Process

The overwhelming fact we must recognize from such a viewpoint is that the basic dynamic of our industrial civilization, since early in the 19th century, has been in the direction of population concentration and

24

"metropolitanization," at the cost of rural communities and provincial towns, cities, and regions, no matter where they are located nor what their cultural derivation.

In the U.S.A., this dynamic has accelerated the decay, or worked against the economic maturation, of major provinces of the nation as diverse as old New England industrial and farming regions, the entire eastern Appalachian backbone, huge sections of the West, Middle West, and South, and countless lesser "pockets of poverty" scattered throughout the land. People of Anglo-Saxon, Scotch-Irish, Scandinavian, African, Middle-European, or Spanish extraction have been equally affected by this process. Most of the current furor about the "plight of our cities" is caused on the one hand by the inability of the few metropolitan sectors, where opportunity is supposedly concentrated, to absorb the overwhelming influx of displaced persons from depressed rural or provincial areas and, on the other hand, by the inability of the stranded towns and cities in those same depressed areas to maintain themselves as going communities.

This phenomenon is, of course, not limited to the United States and is even further advanced in numerous foreign countries. "The Highlands of Scotland," writes a contributor in 1944 to the *Journal of the London School of Economics,* "is a derelict area where geological denudation finds a parallel in the disappearance of population . . . The younger members of the population are tending to disappear as they reach the last years of school age, and the rising standard of living accelerates the movement . . . The process of economic, sociological, and cultural deterioration can be found in almost every corner of Scotland . . ."*

A 1961 report by an international committee of European agricultural experts and economists comments, "After the second world war, the mountain regions of Austria, Germany, Italy, and Yugoslavia were recognized as priority targets for emergency aid . . . The tendency of the Alpine population to age because of the exodus of the young to cities and industrial centers is a special and particularly aggravated form of the exodus

*   **"The Highlands of Scotland: Proposals for Development,"** Hugh Quigley, Agenda of the London School of Economics and Political Science, v. 3, 1944.

from the countryside . . . Mountain regions are depressed areas from the economic standpoint . . ."*

The French historian Aries wrote a generation ago, "A whole section of the population of the Savoy Alps used to live in the forest, but in the second half of the 19th century, the forest was closed off . . . the population was deprived not only of work, but of a reason for existing . . . the inhabitants left . . ."**

Examples of this universal process of rural and provincial disintegration, paired with a corresponding urban hypertrophy, can be drawn from every corner of the world. It affects lands as diverse as England, India, Thailand, Peru, Brazil, or Haiti. In some of these lands, it approaches the dimensions of a national calamity. The process works impartially in Mao's China, in Soviet Russia, in monarchist Ethiopia, in parliamentarian Canada.

The trend is so powerful and universal that generations of people of almost all ideological persuasions have come to regard it as virtually synonymous with progress. Economic theory has rationalized it in terms of the flow of capital into areas of maximum productivity, with a resulting most effective utilization of scientific technology. Industrial and managerial practice has facilitated it, and a great deal of scientific research has been directed to meeting its demands. Public policy has expedited it. Banking and financial tactics support it. Education has dedicated itself almost exclusively to preparing and training the oncoming generation for its requirements. Highway systems are being continually designed, redesigned, built, and rebuilt to meet the ever-increasing traffic loads it generates. Enormous sums are expended and serious environmental risks are accepted to open up new sources of energy to meet its fantastically increasing power demands. The entire fabric of social organization, values, and motivations has adapted to the conditions of life this hyper-urbanizing trend imposes.

*   **"Rural Problems in the Alpine Region,"** Food and Agricultural Organization of the United Nations, 1961.

**   **"Histoire des Populations Francaises,"** Philippe Aries, 1948.

The Long Confrontation

The impact of this trend on non- or proto-industrial folk or agrarian societies throughout the world is well documented over the nearly 200 years since the commercial and industrial revolution began to spread out from the coreland of northwestern Europe in the latter 18th century. A characteristic sequence of effects has repetitiously accompanied this impact, as follows:

1. The disruption of localized, relatively self-sufficient economies, with their supporting technologies and logistic arrangements.

2. Expropriation of land and other natural resources from tribal, peasant, yeoman, or local aristocratic ownership, and their concentration in larger units for machine-intensive management capable of maximizing export surpluses and yield on investment.

3. Monetization of local exchange to replace distribution of goods at least partially through barter or through customary arrangements sanctioned by family, tribe, or religion.

4. Dislodgement of dispersed agricultural or pastoral populations, with a resulting influx to the cities, a rapid increase in the urban proletariat, and an accelerating rate of urbanization.

5. A resulting disintegration of communities, folkways, skills, and life styles which crystallized around, supported, and embellished the traditional modes of livelihood. This process inevitably involved the disruption of deep-seated patterns of work, sacrament, and attachment to homeland, and has been responsible for much of the disorientation, apathy, or anger which marks the psychology of what we currently speak of as "disadvantaged minorities." (That this sort of collective trauma is essentially due to derangement of customary patterns of livelihood and life style, rather than to clashes of purely linguistic or ethnic dichotomies, is well evidenced by its repeated historical occurrence *within* nations of relatively homogenous culture and language. England, in the days of the early textile mill boom and the Luddite uprisings, is an example.)

We may note, in passing, that almost from its beginnings in Europe, these effects of industrialism on traditional societies were trenchantly criticized in humanitarian terms by individuals such as Dickens, Ruskin, and

Zola. They were also resisted physically by generally ineffective peasant, clan, or petty-national protests and Jacqueries everywhere. Much of the history of the 19th century is, in fact, the chronicle of how these resistances were overcome through a combination of financial and commercial leverage, entrepreneurial energy, military might, missionary zeal, and the sheer impressiveness of scientific technology in action. The resultant of this combination of factors was that, over the past two centuries, countless minor folk and agrarian societies in virtually all corners of the globe were obliterated, and countless millions of rural and provincial dwellers abandoned their farms, villages, towns, and minor cities to migrate (all too often) to the slums of the nearest metropolis or industrial center.

This entire syndrome characterizing the impact of industrialism on traditional societies has been observed and described in the Hispanic Rockies at least since the 1930s, as our preceding historical resumé indicates. The first obvious comment we may make in the light of this perspective is that the economic stalemate in northern New Mexico is clearly no local phenomenon, explicable in terms of politics or ethnic relationships within the region itself. It is rather a close-at-hand instance of a socioeconomic process of worldwide provenance and import and one whose ramifications reach through the entire fabric of our society.

The Problems of Metropolitanization

The very universality of this trend tempts us to accept it as inevitable. There is indeed a rationalization of long-standing respectability ready at hand to justify this conclusion. The socioeconomic deterioration of "bypassed" backward societies and communities, according to this rationalization, is a transitional effect — the sad but necessary price of progress towards scientific civilization. When the transition is completed, when the necessary regrouping into the new era urban-industrial complexes is achieved and the essential re-education and re-training of the people perfected, the full benefits of industrially generated affluence will begin to flow, and mankind will reach a new plateau of wellbeing and material abundance. In the meantime, the disruption and demoralization of old and sentimentally valued ways of life is to be regretted. Such painful experiences

28

should be tempered as much as possible by enlightened eleemosynary and public policies, but the all-important process of assimilation and acculturation is the only final answer and should be expedited in every possible way.

During the earlier formative stages of this process, this formulation of the ethics and praxis of industrialization (for which term "colonization" might, of course, be substituted in very many cases) could remain plausible, if only on the basis of benefits to be realized in the not-too-distant future. Humanitarian objections could be set aside as the well-intentioned but impractical gestures of romantics not in touch with the stern but just operations of the economic world.

In recent decades, however, and especially in the period since the close of World War II, the entire rationalization is on the verge of breakdown. The slow historical "drift to the cities" has accelerated into a dismaying proliferation, worldwide in extent, of urban slums, ghettos, *barriadas, favelas*, and the like, mostly populated by the residues of demolished rural and provincial communities and societies. This proliferation has vividly demonstrated the widespread inability of contemporary industrial economies to integrate uprooted masses into their systems in any useful, humane, or ecologically sound way. The arsenal of technological wizardries at the command of these economies has spectacularly failed to alleviate the results of this trend.

The drain on natural resources — fossil fuels, soils, forests, ores, waters, now even the atmosphere itself — imposed by the gigantic logistic mechanisms necessary to maintain these non-productive but cancerously growing agglomerations of humanity even at the bare subsistence level, threatens to overwhelm our hopes for mankind's future. The psychic strain engendered by the overcrowding, deprivation, and frustration of the new superghettos has already generated massive civil disturbances and promises greater ones to come. At the same time, the bypassed and semi-abandoned rural and provincial regions from which the new urban masses come, continue to decay, deteriorate, and spread.

29

Urban-Industrial Civilization in Crisis

Dysfunctions of this magnitude and severity strongly suggest that the processes of industrialization and urbanization, as we have experienced them since before the Civil War, will certainly not resolve the problems of our Southern Rocky Mountain microcosm any more than they have resolved those of scores of similar provinces and lands around the globe.

It seems a tragic circumstance that most of our accumulated "conventional wisdom," as it bears on economic progress and technological development, leads only to intensification of trends that contain the seeds of self-destruction. The classic formulas calling for mass production and mass merchandising, for capital-intensive mechanization and automation, for massive public investment in "social infrastructure," and for massive corporate investment in machinery and plant are, after all, operative only where they can recreate or intensify the megalopolitan environment, with all its entrainment of increasingly unmanageable problems.

The fact seems to be that urban-industrial civilization itself — under whatever political ideology it operates — is entering a transitional, if not a crisis, phase. The computer-borne projections of the economists, demographers, and planners of all nations, with their foreshadowings of unprecedented population congestion, natural-resources depletion, mass famines, land-water-and-air pollution, and the like, are deeply disquieting indications of uncertainties ahead.

Characteristics of a New Pattern of Development

Viewing the socioeconomic situation of a region such as the uplands in this perspective, certain challenging theses present themselves for consideration, as, for example:

1. It is no longer possible to "solve the problems" of such a regional community by expediting wholesale outmigration and assimilation of its population into the urban, metropolitan, or industrial areas of the nation. We have probably some time ago passed the point of diminishing returns on this process which is now generating more and graver difficulties for society as a whole than it resolves.

2. Neither is it possible to rehabilitate provincial regions such as the uplands by importing big industry and its works. The dominant

30

characteristic of modern primary and extractive industry (including "agribusiness"), geared to the national market, is labor-conservative, machine-intensive, and moving towards maximum automation. Very large investments are required per job created (e.g., $175,000 for a modern pulp mill). Regions dominated by such industries tend to depopulate except for company towns of varying degrees of cultural and social impoverishment, or else to integrate with the nearest interurban industrial complex, and hence to take on the degenerative tendencies of megalopolis.

3. Correlatively, the bulk of the livelihood needs of such a region must be met within the region itself by skilled, scientific, intensive, and conservative use of the lands, waters, and renewable biotic and environmental resources of the region. The long-term strategy for economic development should be gradual de-involvement from the mass logistic machinery of the continental economy, with its enormous and ever-increasing consumption of energy and irreplaceable natural resources. This de-involvement should be facilitated by an evolution towards basic self-sufficiency at a high real standard of living.

4. Such an evolution calls for a new technological, agricultural, and industrial orientation, stressing small-scaled and diversified primary production, adapted to the land and natural resources pattern of the region, to the ecologic balance and health of the total biotic community, and to the needs of a decentralized and dispersed population of effective and vital small communities. This type of productive economy will be manpower-, skill-, and science-intensive, rather than capital-, energy-, and machine-intensive. It will maximize economies of site and logistic relationships, rather than economies of scale.

There is good reason to urge that much in the demographic pattern, the livelihood tradition, and the cultural heritage of the uplands community favors this type of economic evolution. In Part Two, we shall attempt to outline the philosophy and rationale of policy in such fields as land and resources management, education, technological and agricultural research, public facilities planning, and community organization which will expedite this evolution. For convenience, we shall term this philosophy and rationale "ecologic development planning."

31

PART TWO
GOALS FOR REGIONAL DEVELOPMENT

PART TWO

GOALS FOR REGIONAL DEVELOPMENT

In order to pursue further the concept of "ecological" development for a region such as the northern New Mexico uplands, let us accept for the present the generalized characteristics of such a development pattern as summarized at the close of Part One.

A logical next step would be to attempt to interpret this pattern somewhat more concretely in terms of potentials (and hence, opportunities) for economic, technical, and social evolution within the regional community. A preliminary inventory of such evolutionary potentials might look something like this:

POTENTIAL I: **A full complement of region-supplying primary industries.**

It is becoming increasingly obvious that much of the machinery and methodology of big industry, big agriculture, big commerce, and big transportation is functionally inappropriate to the real needs of the inhabitants of regions and provinces that are neither metropolitan nor agro-

35

industrial. Where such operations are introduced into such areas (usually for the advantage of remote interests), the natural and human balance of life is usually adversely affected and depopulation, community disintegration, and landscape deterioration commonly result.

Where the need for maximized, export-oriented, and investment-motivated production does not exist, the basic commodity and service requirements of a life- and community-oriented non-metropolitan regional community can, to a large extent, be handled by relatively simple, small, and medium-scaled plant and process, by modest public facilities, and by uncomplex local social arrangements. "Inefficiencies," due to diseconomies of scale in individual productive operations, can be more than compensated for by vastly simplified logistical relationships and by freedom from parasitical costs of financing, over-transportation, over-handling of commodities, and over-administration of services.

A regional technology and production pattern of this type should be fostered in every possible way by public and private policy, research, education, and training. It derives naturally from traditional values and expectations and can be effectively implemented through individual enterprise and community consensus when freed from the confusion of extraneous controls and pressures and the restrictions of monopolistic practices. Efficient, low-cost, small- and medium-scale production and distribution of a broad range of basic necessaries of life, produced from local land, mineral, and biotic resources, is ecologic here in the senses that:

1. It derives from and grows out of the underlying livelihood tradition and "know-how" of a community long versed in the utilization of this land and its products.

2. It is adapted to the scale and occurrence-pattern of the resources of a mountainous terrain where arable land, timber, water, and minerals are dispersed in small pockets generally unsuited for mass exploitation.

3. It is less subject to the pressure for continuous maximum output that is characteristic of large heavily capitalized industries and that is responsible for much of the over-exploitation of land, fossil fuel, and biotic resources that have characterized such industries.

4. It is less dependent upon massive transportation and energy conversion installations and operations which are destructive of the natural environment.

5. It diverts a higher proportion of its budget to skilled manpower activities rather than to larger resource-consuming installations and operations.

POTENTIAL II: **Land- and skill-intensive agriculture and husbandry.**

Much destructive use of agricultural and pastoral land within the uplands, as in many physiographically similar parts of the nation and the world, is due to the attempt to compete on the general market in cash-crop field farming and stock raising on farms and ranches too small or too inaccessible. At the same time, large quantities of high-value vegetables, fruits, dairy and poultry products, etc., are imported into the region and must be paid for out of the meager cash earnings of such farms and ranches. The result is often soil depletion, symbiotic degeneration, prolonged economic decline, and progressive abandonment of homesteads. This situation has been more or less continuously discussed in many reports since the 1930s.

A shift in the direction of a high-level subsistence and regional specialty market agriculture would obviously improve the nutritional, health, and economic status of the rural segment of the regional community. Such a shift would be "ecological" in the senses that:

1. It reduces the demand for bulk output of livestock and monocultural crops produced at minimum labor costs and so reduces the chances for soil depletion, erosion, etc.

2. It justifies higher labor inputs on agricultural land and so increases the chances for scientific and conservative management.

3. It grows non-traumatically out of the earlier usages of the regional communities and relates feasibly to the patterns of irrigable land distribution and tenure.

POTENTIAL III: **Deep functional involvement of the community in soil and biotic conservation.**

This component of the desired developmental trend is obviously

37

"ecological" in character. The objective here is the attainment of a mode of livelihood in which conservative and regenerative use of the natural environment is an integral part of economic activity and folkways and mores rather than a doctrine imposed externally by bureaucratic regulation. For this to be possible, local communities must continue to evolve in civic, managerial, technical, and entrepreneurial competence. Income- and subsistence-generating activities must be tied in an increasingly direct and functional fashion with the intelligent use of the full range of environmental resources such that the proper care and regeneration of these resources become a matter of ordinary prudence, common sense, good housekeeping, and day-to-day ethics.

Essential to such an evolution is a general understanding of the fact that much — perhaps most — of good "environmental housekeeping" in rural, wildlands, and uplands terrains is dependent on intelligent and motivated personal human effort. It cannot be effectively carried out by mechanical operations and bureaucratic directives. A deep sense of participation and pride in skilled personal and group achievement and an attachment to and appreciation of the land, backed up by a justified expectation of solid economic benefit, must be present to motivate such individual and community involvement in environmental improvement.

POTENTIAL IV: **Enriched village-community economic, social, and cultural life.**

It is obvious that a general rise in the level of diversified and complimentary productive activity, intra-regional exchange, and indigenous technical specializations based on local natural resources utilization will require the continuous improvement of numerous regional "microurban" centers as places of residence close to areas of work, as focal points of circulation, coordination, and exchange, and as cultural, educational, and social milieus. This improvement must express itself in increasing sophistication of architecture, site development, and public facilities planning, and in a progressive establishment or re-establishment of a range of locality-serving institutions within villages — schools, cultural facilities,

38

mercados, workshops, co-ops, and administrative meeting rooms and offices, inns and *posadas*, sports fields, etc.

The existing constellation of villages and hamlets provides the logical and strategic base for such an evolution and much of the cultural tradition to fortify it.

In a sense, this is the culminating objective of the entire process under discussion, as it is precisely the impoverishment of local social and economic life which is causing the decay and depopulation of so many provincial regions throughout the nation and the globe, as summed up in Part One.

This pattern of development is "ecological" in the senses that it:

1. Derives from the regional life and livelihood style and from the long-established pattern of settlement and land use.

2. Works against the prevailing process of rural cultural, economic, and population erosion which is the underlying cause of dysfunctional over-urbanization, social disorganization, and environmental deterioration at the national level.

3. Locates population in effective logistic relationship to the key natural resources of the region and minimizes wasteful over-transportation and other resource-consuming operations.

4. Facilitates a skill- and manpower-intensive management of land and biotic resources such as is necessary for their proper conservation and rehabilitation, by reducing parasitical and unnecessary social overhead and infrastructure costs.

5. Places people in a direct, creative, and mutually beneficial working relationship with the natural cycles and life processes of the region in a manner conducive to general health and well–being, both physical, intellectual, and spiritual.

We may now examine, at a somewhat more concrete and specific level, various activities, agencies, public policies and programs, institutions, and institutional arrangements operative within the region and attempt to assess them in relation to their effect, positive or negative, on the regional potentials identified above.

(There is good reason to believe that similar factors will be found operative in the many "disadvantaged" rural and provincial territories throughout the nation and the world.)

39

This assessment will be, of necessity, philosophic. It will be directed towards the underlying doctrine and rationale governing these various operative factors and will view them in the perspective of the large issues outlined in Part One. Specific recommendations or solutions will generally not be offered. It is intended, rather that some basic questions will be raised, unintended consequences of some policies and actions pointed out, inadequately realized alternative lines of action suggested, and neglected fields of concern and consideration outlined. Since an unusually large fraction (about 65%) of the land and biotic resources of this region are directly controlled by one or another of various government agencies, bureaucratic and administrative policy will, of necessity, figure correspondingly in the comments.

The discussion will be frankly subjective and not much pretense will be made of statistical proof and scholarly documentation, although references will be cited where feasible. It is hoped that this approach will stimulate some searching re-examination of the objectives of public and semi-public policies in this remarkable microcosm of the southern Rockies. Such a re-examination may, in turn, eventually contribute towards a body of public planning and policy-coordinating techniques which will allow this regional community to work out its unique potentials.

For convenience, the four "potentials" described above will be examined in order. Factors affecting each will be assessed in the following categories:

Customary usage
Land and resources management (governmental)
Education
Public facilities planning
The entrepreneurial environment (public and semi-public fiscal, legal, and commercial controls)
Community modes of organization
Technical and agricultural research

The remainder of Part Two will be devoted to the proposed examination and assessment.

40

POTENTIAL I: **A full complement of region-supplying primary industries.**

Customary usage — In common with practically all "underdeveloped" and "bypassed" enclaves and provinces of the nation, northern New Mexico is markedly deficient in the conventionally defined "primary" or "basic" industries. A disproportionately large share of monetary income within the region comes from government employment, exported labor, and "transfer" funds. There is considerable import even of relatively simple goods which might obviously be produced within the region such as processed meats, breadstuffs, and other food products. This deficiency has been much discussed and is commonly attributed to shortage of investment capital, inadequate markets and labor pools, insufficient natural resources and raw materials, lack of technical and entrepreneurial ability, and transportation barriers. *

Counterbalancing this "statistically visible" condition, however, it should be realized that a great deal of true "primary" production is carried on in the uplands outside the regular commercial channels, particularly in the form of home, farm, and family growing and processing of food-stuffs and in the construction of residential, farm, and other buildings. Complementarily, much distribution of the results of this industry is handled through barter and through kinship networks. This type of localized non-commercial industry and exchange is difficult to estimate but probably constitutes a considerably more important part of regional economic activity than is realized. The existence of this economic "subsystem" undoubtedly has a great deal to do with the unusual resistance this regional community has offered to the kind of total impoverishment and socioeconomic erosion that has afflicted many other similar regions of the nation, such as portions of Appalachia. It should be given far more serious attention by those concerned with economic improvement and offers an invaluable base from

* See, for example, New Mexico Studies in Business and Economics, No. 11, **"The Outlook for Food Processing by Small New Mexico Firms,"** Bureau of Business Research, University of New Mexico, May 1963.

which a more sophisticated, regionally adapted production and exchange system may evolve. In contradistinction to the term "primary" in conventional economic usage, we might describe the system as the sector of "regional subsistence" industry.

Land and resources management (governmental) — Probably this factor exerts the strongest influence on the growth of region-serving industry through the large Federal agencies managing wildlands and their biotic populations. Of these agencies, the U.S. Forest Service is the most influential, since it has jurisdiction over about 2.9 million acres within the region, or about 35% of its total surface. * The importance of this jurisdiction is greater than the percentage suggests, as this area represents the cream of timber and recreational resources. Other Federal and State agencies control an additional one-third.

The possibility of an entire range of local industries based on wood harvesting, processing, and byproducts utilization, and also on various types of recreational management and development would seem obviously quite dependent upon policies exercised by these dominant agencies, particularly the U.S. Forest Service. Data gathered for the 1960 census indicates that only 7% of regional "primary" employment was generated by forest management, timber harvesting, and wood products processing, a surprisingly low figure for a region noted for its mantle of forest.** To assess the relationship of Federal agency policies to this condition is a complex and controversial task since disputes of long standing, such as that between large timber and stockraising interests and the forest custodians, or over the priority of local

o

* **"Agricultural Land and Water in New Mexico,"** State Planning Office, 1966.

** **"Development Potentials of the Northern New Mexico Uplands,"** Peter van Dresser, 1962.

vs. national public interest, are involved. However, in the light of the special criteria adopted for this discussion, the following comments may be offered:

The resultant of official policy controlling timber harvesting in northern New Mexico's forests has included a movement towards larger operating organizations, more massive machinery, and more centralized processing plants (saw and planing mills). This movement is, of course, the logical expression of the financial and economic forces shaping all large extractive industry. Through maximum mechanization and elimination of manpower, and through the centralization of all possible processing and remanufacturing operations in distant urban areas, it leads to the typical effects on the people and landscape of the region discussed in Part One — e.g., depopulation, community disintegration, and physical environmental deterioration.

It would seem we should now be asking questions such as:

• Is another form of technological and economic progress imaginable in this vital field which will reinforce rather than undermine the human and natural ecology of the region?

• Can we, for example, achieve a "vertical integration" of a full range of forest- and wildlands-based industries here adapted through careful design and planning to the landforms and resources-pattern of the area, and carried out in true partnership with the indigenous communities?

• Can we gradually complement big-machine-intensive exploitation of the forests with people-, skill-, and science-intensive care and utilization? Can we, in this way, increase many times over the value added within the region through true multiple use of a much wider range of resources, through the production of more finished and more valuable products and services, and through the provision of high-level subsistence to a considerably increased regional population? May we not actually, in the long run, thus increase in absolute terms the gross forest output of materials, services, and amenities needful to the national economy while maintaining its optimum ecological health?

The time may be ripe for some bold rethinking of Forest Service and kindred policies, including types of benefit-cost analysis responsive to the mounting social and economic burden of rural community erosion, and types of contractual arrangements more encouraging to local enterprise and community participation. The bible of the forest custodians, the Forest Service Manual, says, ". . . The national forests will be made available for public use and enjoyment, insofar as this is consistent with over-all management of the national forests for the greatest public good . . . management of the various resources will be determined through specific analysis and weighing of all relevant factors."

A study published by the Fund for the Republic comments on this proviso as follows: *

> Thus the Service recognized, in the matter-of-fact pages of its manual, that its ultimate job is nothing less than the definition of "the public good," a task once reserved for philosopher-kings. This is the tremendous responsibility that Congress has delegated to all the forest agencies, and with it the power to determine the very character of the American land. The great danger is that an entrenched professional bureaucracy will become shortsighted in its perception of the public good . . .

It is certainly possible that we are due a considerably broader understanding of what constitutes the "public good," both local and national, in this sphere of resources-management in the New Mexico uplands.

Education — The content and policy of public education, including technical and vocational training, has a pervasive influence on a possible trend towards the evolution of a regionally oriented industrial complex in northern New Mexico. Here again we encounter a much disputed topic. Some general observations may be offered, however, again in the light of the special purposes of this discussion.

Broadly speaking, it can hardly be challenged that the educational establishment has "bought" the idea that opportunity for the oncoming

---

* **"Bureaucracy and the Forests,"** Charles A. Reich, Fund for the Republic, 1962.

generation lies overwhelmingly in cities and urban areas and in the specialized commercial, "service," and "new technology" jobs located there. This, of course, is particularly true of "vo-tech" training where electronics, business machines, computers, automation, advanced metalworking, automotive technology, aircraft and astronautic engineering, etc., are the glamor subjects. Virtually no institutions are devoted to research and training in small-scale village and rural technology and related scientific resources management and utilization. Even our schools of agriculture have long since converted themselves to schools of "agribusiness" and pay only token attention to the technical problems of villagers and smallholders. The only exception to this seems to be a residual and dwindling part of Extension Service activities concerned with home economics and home food processing. Even these subjects, however, are being converted to education in "consumership."

Besides this specific bias in curriculum content, the general attitudes and policies of professional educators and educational administrators are frankly urban-oriented. As rapidly as possible, village schools are being consolidated and located in the nearest and largest available town or city. Also as rapidly as possible, school buildings and plant are being rebuilt in the latest fashions of synthetic materials, windowless, plastic-paneled, prefabricated, and asphalt-surrounded, prototyping the world of 1984. Urban skills, behavior, dress, rewards, and goals are set up in these insulated, sterile micro-environments as desirable and exclusive models for youthful development.

Such an educational milieu obviously provides neither skills nor incentive for the intelligent understanding and use of regional natural resources and environment. In view of the near bankruptcy and lack of opportunity of our over-burdened metropolitan areas, an educational philosophy which still concentrates exclusively on preparing young people technically for life and employment within them deserves at the least very careful scrutiny. The work of institutions such as the Danish Folk Schools, the Rural Universities of India, Berea College in the Appalachians, Warren Wilson College in North Carolina, and the Escuela Agricola Panamericana in Honduras might provide useful landmarks in such a scrutiny.

Public facilities planning — Possibly the most direct impact within this category of factors on the status of region- serving primary industry is that of road planning and construction. For the encouragement of localized production and exchange of basic commodities and services, there is needed an effective and relatively dense *intra-regional* network of all-weather roads. Such a network should be designed to provide convenient access between the various resource-type areas within the region and between the numerous villages in which economic and social activity is to be encouraged. These highways should be as inexpensive as possible and engineered for relatively light traffic and moderate speeds.

Present highway policy, both State and Federal, is almost completely the reverse of this. Even so-called secondary or "farm-to-market" roads must now be engineered with such high standards of cross-section, gradients, etc., that they are equivalent to the major highways of a few years ago and cost an average of $100,000 per mile. (This condition is, of course, aggravated in mountainous terrain.)

As for primary and interstate roads, these are notoriously so expensive that only the most major through-routes connecting cities can be financed, and these only by earmarking a disproportionately large fraction of State funds for them, multiplied by heavy Federal subsidy. It is rationalized that two or three such routes traversing the uplands region will "develop" it economically. This is an extremely dubious assumption, as experience indicates that such high-speed throughways tend to attr.ct a very narrow range of traffic-servicing industries (truck stops, chain motels, and chain eating places) which distribute very little economic benefits to surrounding areas. Highspeed throughways, commonly indeed, abet area economic demoralization through increasing local dependency upon distant urban centers. Thus they often constitute publicly subsidized handicaps to the development of localized region-serving industries.

This is glaringly the case as regards the emergence of a true regionally based and regionally oriented recreation industry. The uplands, as a sort of potential Switzerland in the Southwest, are well adapted to vacation-visitor enjoyment through a multiplicity of small inns, lodges, *posadas*, hostelries, and the like, adapted to the special characteristics of the local settings. Such facilities can be financed, constructed, and operated by local enterprise and

46

can distribute tourist income most widely and beneficially to the people of the region.

Facilities of this kind will attract a special sector of tourism — i.e., people interested in relatively long-term vacation residence within the region and in leisurely exploration and enjoyment of its various seasons and aspects. For such usage, a diversity of minor scenic roads is required, offering a wide variety of destinations and interconnections. Large volumes of fast traffic need not be handled on such a system, yet the tourist revenue yield per passenger mile will be far greater than for major routes due to the considerably longer average stopover period. (Under current conditions, the average stopover lasts from one to three nights only.) Present road policies thus tend to choke off the possibilities for a far more efficient and locally beneficial type of recreational industry by signally failing to provide adequate internal circulation routes.

Another sector of public facilities planning practice which adversely affects the development of local industry has to do with the construction of public buildings. Though northern New Mexico is famous for a long and honorable tradition of incorporating simple indigenous material in a distinctive and functional architecture, the trend towards the use of pre-fab and standardized imported materials for schools and various public structures is gaining throughout the region. Justification for this practice by school boards and other agencies is, of course, budget economy — the higher costs per square foot of the traditionally built structures.

Yet this superficial accounting does not measure the full impact of the practice on local employment and income levels. No reckoning is made of the "multiplier" effect of funds expended for local labor rather than for imported labor and pre-manufactured products. No administrative mechanism exists by which agencies might act on such information if it were available.

The cumulative drain of this growing practice on the regional monetary balance of trade may be quite important (not to speak of the loss in cultural and esthetic values and the decline of local technical and entrepreneurial competence). Serious consideration should be given to practices and techniques which might help reverse this trend, amongst which might be: replacement of building and design codes and criteria adopted by national organizations and pressure groups for metropolitan conditions by well-

47

researched codes and criteria adapted to local materials and conditions; more sophisticated design and use of indigenous material; special vocational training in such design and use; encouragement of cooperative building groups; and better integration of communities with administrative agencies.

The entrepreneurial environment — The intangible climate of tax schedules, corporation regulations, banking policies, employment and sanitary codes, licensing and franchise requirements, etc., etc., within which local productive enterprise must operate is a complex and subtle subject of study. It may reasonably be pointed out here, however, that increasingly this body of social control is conceived and drafted by urban-minded officials and specialists concerned with the problems and complexities of metropolitan areas. The strict application of this entire *corpus* of regulations to small-scale village- and locality-centered productive industry and trade could unnecessarily and unwittingly cripple them.

The ever-mounting complexity of both Federal and State taxing and social security regulations which seem always to work discriminatory hardships on the smaller businessman and entrepreneur has long been the subject of complaint. Similarly, credit policies of banks and of various Federal lending agencies are believed by many to favor conventional larger urban-centered commercial and manufacturing enterprises or "agribusiness" operations in farming, as opposed to innovative, smaller-scaled rural-based enterprises. (Discriminatory drafting and enforcement of sanitary requirements, for example, are held by some investigators to have been a major device in the near-elimination of the small dairy industry throughout the nation. In the Las Vegas vicinity alone, some thirty family dairies went out of business shortly after the licensing in New Mexico of a national milk distributing corporation in the late 1950s. Ironically, the lands utilized by many of these local dairy enterprises are now a part of a Federally financed wildlife sanctuary. This raises an interesting question of comparative value systems. Did the total human ecology of the area gain or lose by this high-level manipulation?)

Many more such practices, unintentional or otherwise, undoubtedly help "load the dice" against the desired development of region-serving

48

primary industries in the uplands. Some efforts are being made to remedy this situation, mainly through education of "small" businessmen and prospective entrepreneurs in the intricacies of management, accounting, and bureaucratic compliance. But it may well be that some of our laws and regulations themselves need revising in the direction of simplicity and adaptability to rural and village conditions. We must recognize that a certain, and probably growing, proportion of these controls is the result of a Parkinsonian process in the bureaucratic world through which the proliferation of regulatory activities and of the careers connected with them becomes an end in itself.

Much more attention might also be paid to devices and institutions more appropriate to productive enterprise in the less highly commercialized and competitive world outside megalopolis such as mutual finance and credit organizations, cooperatives, and marketing associations. Experience and practice in the small Scandinavian countries is highly pertinent to this pattern of economic and industrial evolution.

Community modes of organization — The lack of effective formal modes of community and village organization is very characteristic of the uplands. North of Santa Fé, there are only six municipal corporations in the entire region. Other types of in-community organizations — *acequia* commissions, parish groups, insurance and burial societies, domestic water associations, local cattle growers' associations — are sharply limited in their interests and activities. Kinship ties tend to ramify throughout the region rather than to center around geographically defined communities.* No institutions comparable to the township meetings of early New England, the Councils of Village Elders in India, or the *cabildos, aldeas,* and *patronatos* of Latin American countries are to be found. Thus, while the physical pattern of hamlets and villages is well defined throughout the region, it is not reinforced by a corresponding pattern of localized social or economic institutions.

---

* **"Settlement Patterns of the Chama Valley,"** Doctoral Dissertation, Frances Swadesh, University of Colorado, 1964.

This lack probably retards the growth of an adequate set of regional productive and exchange facilities more sophisticated than can be handled through informal family and kinship arrangements. For example, while a good deal of local and regional produce is distributed by "pickup truck peddlers" and seasonal roadside stands, the village *mercado*, which provides the focal point for local trade throughout most of Latin America, functions only vestigially in the uplands, and then primarily for tourist patronage.

Correspondingly, the lack of public facilities within the villages, such as could be provided by more effective local organizations (reliable water supply and sewage disposal systems, schools, clinics, recreational and cultural facilities, etc.) works against the establishment of decentralized small industries within them.

It might be pointed out that this deficiency is not a part of the cultural heritage of the settlers of this region. Villages of the mountain and seacoast provinces of 17th and 18th century Spain, from which many of the New World colonists came, actually possessed a wide variety of social and economic institutions maintained by the community.*

The mode of political organization imposed on the regional community by English-American law, with its emphasis on the county as the unit of rural government, probably does little to remedy this deficiency, diffusing authority as it does over large and frequently loosely knit areas. Municipal incorporation, under this same body of law, tends to be too ponderous for the needs of village and hamlet dwellers, and is too tied in with the intricacies of State-level finance and politics. Serious consideration should be given to arrangements and devices which may provide adequate channels of essential community action towards economic self-development in the uplands.

Technical and agricultural research — For several generations the bias of technical "R & D" in the United States has been strongly in the direction of ever-larger industrial operating units, more heavily mechanized

---

* See, for example, **"The Spanish Labyrinth,"** Gerald Brennan, Cambridge University Press, 1950.

and capitalized volume production, and more elaborate merchandizing, processing, and packaging of all commodities for mass urban markets. An entire spectrum of alternative techniques for decentralized, skill- and labor-intensive basic production at the family, community, and local level has been neglected as a result of this bias. Traditional methods and processes have been forgotten and the tools and equipment appropriate to them have gone out of production while new developments in small-scale and "intermediate" technology evolved mostly in foreign countries have been ignored.*

Appropriate research and training programs in this sphere, including forest products utilization, intensive agriculture and horticulture, food and plant products, building with indigenous materials, textiles, furniture and equipment, recreational installations, community utilities and facilities are all needed with particular focus on the uplands region, its natural resources, and its economy. Existing institutions carry on such work only in the most token and marginal fashion. The very location of most of them — in the larger towns and cities of the plains portion of the State — bars them from contact with and appreciation of the special problems, challenges, and opportunities of the northern New Mexico environment. Their economic and technological orientation is strongly towards large-scale commercialized field agriculture or major "basic" industrial development. These existing institutions tend to build their curricula around the sophisticated space- and cybernetic-age subjects and around liberal arts erudition competitive with the scholastic standards and fashions of the national academic scene. Correspondingly, such vocational training as is offered focuses on trades and skills considered appropriate to the employment opportunities which are supposed to exist in the nation's metropolitan centers. Some means of compensating effectively for this bias is indicated if we are to create an environment for appropriate industrial development in the uplands.

* "The Massive Market for Simplicity," *British Industry Week*, April 25, 1969; also "Teaching People to Help Themselves," *The Commonwealth Journal*, April 1966; and also "Intermediate Technologies," *Development Digest*, January 1969.

POTENTIAL II: **Skill- and land-intensive agriculture and husbandry.**

Customary usage — As discussed in Part One, the uplands settlements were for centuries virtually self-sufficient in food production, albeit in terms of a simple, yet reasonably adequate, diet emphasizing corn, beans, chili, squash, etc., and locally raised beef, mutton, and chevron. It may be fairly stated that the higher attainments of plant culture were not particularly strong points in the Spanish tradition, and local specializations based on this skill never evolved on a wide scale in New Mexico. (The early Franciscan mission communities might be cited as an exception, but their example did not seem to set the patterns in the uplands.) This deficiency persists and commercial contact with the rest of the continent has not so much stimulated the development of local specialty agriculture and food industries as made the region dependent on outside sources to satisfy increasingly cosmopolitan tastes.

The total acreage of irrigated lands within the uplands is estimated by the State Engineer Office at 168,000 or roughly 1.1 per inhabitant. This is ample to supply the vegetable, fruit, and cereal requirements of the entire regional population including Santa Fé and Los Alamos at a high nutritional standard if levels of productivity per acre equal to average good farming practice throughout the nation are attained in the region.* Frequent reference is made to the small size of farm holdings within the region (due to the subdivision by inheritance) as militating against efficient agriculture. This is not inevitable, as some of the highest per acre productions in the world are attained on intensively worked small holdings in countries where the necessary skills have been developed and maintained.

On this basis, an additional 125,000 acres would then be available for feed production for dairy animals and poultry. This estimate disregards the possibility of bringing new irrigated land within the region into use —

---

* Based on the need for 1.2 production acres per family of four, as adapted from production and consumption tables by Louis Herzog, U.S. Department of Agriculture's statistical sources. **"Democracy's Answer to Communism,"** William-Frederick Press, New York, 1955.

52

ultimately as much as 700,000 acres, as estimated in the current Rio Grande basin survey carried out by an interagency research team of the Department of Agriculture.* It also disregards the large meat supply available from improved non-irrigated stock range management, provided its yield were channeled into regional markets rather than exported.

Thus, although the earlier traditions of the uplands are favorable to regional self-containment in the matter of food production (and though these traditions still persist to a considerable degree), substantial effort will be required to make up for the failure of a more sophisticated agriculture to evolve within the region over the past two or three generations. Determined individual and community exertions, supported by appropriate public policies, will be necessary if this sort of change is to be realized.

Land and resources management (governmental) — As mentioned in Part One, about 65% of the total land surface of the uplands is controlled by governmental agencies, largely the U.S. Forest Service, but also the Federal Bureau of Land Management, the State Land Office, and a few others. These lands consist mostly of forest, wildlands, grazing, and chapparal terrains. Most of the more fertile and watered valleys (totaling perhaps half a million acres, or 6% of all lands) are in the hands of private owners, and government policies do not directly dictate the type of agriculture practiced on them.

However, the use and management of flowing waters (and, to an increasing extent, subsurface waters) throughout the region is subject to rather rigorous public control. Irrigation water traditionally used by the nearly 600 community, village, and pueblo *acequia* systems in the uplands is "frozen" for such use by the doctrine of prior appropriation for beneficial use, administered through the State Engineer Office. The amount of such appropriation is being clarified by the Hydrographic Survey conducted by this Office, as confirmed by agreement with local users or by adjudication when necessary. The total amount presently may be roughly estimated at three-quarters of a million acre-feet per year, at the very highest.

In addition to this traditionally confirmed use, however, a large portion

---

*   See **"Water and Related Land Resources,"** reports of Upper Rio Grande Basin, U.S. Department of Agriculture and State Engineer, 1968 and 1969.

53

of the surface flow precipitated in or passing through the uplands (from southern Colorado) has been pre-empted since New Mexico arrived at statehood through the establishment of a number of major downstream irrigation projects such as the Middle Rio Grande Irrigation District (1925), the Elephant Butte District (1915), and others still farther downstream in Texas and Mexico. The allotment of water amongst these various projects is determined by several interstate agreements such as the Rio Grande Compact (1938) and the Upper Colorado River Compact (1948). Probably an average of at least three-quarters of the waters flowing into or running off the New Mexico uplands leave the region for downstream use in accordance with geographic patterns of irrigation recognized by these compacts.

Probably the chief effect of this complex of controls on the possibilities for more sophisticated irrigation-agriculture practices in the uplands is the legal and fiscal complications they place in the way of stabilizing seasonal local water supplies through the use of small upstream dams and various runoff-retarding and infiltration-increasing practices. Such techniques are subject to challenge since they may affect the delivery of water quotas to downstream users under the compacts. The resulting legal and engineering disputes are costly and time-consuming, and their resolution is usually beyond the ability of village and community water users to finance. As a result, water shortages are common in most uplands irrigation systems in the latter summer and early fall and this risk discourages many small farmers from putting in higher value crops not resistant to drought.

This effect is reinforced by the practice of various key agencies of:

1. evaluating economic benefits and hence the "feasibility" of irrigation improvements mainly in terms of increased yields of conventional cash crops; and

2. designing such improvements for contract construction at relatively large scale and high monetary costs, rather than as staged projects adapted to the technical capacities and income levels of the regional communities.

While in recent years there has been some attempt to modify the first practice by recognizing "side benefits" such as recreation and general area economic improvement, much remains to be done in the way of recognizing the value of intensive subsistence agriculture as essential to a self-supporting regional community. Such a community, in turn, offers the most effective

54

means of utilizing the entire spectrum of natural resources on a skill and manpower basis. Present accounting techniques are insensitive to the large range of social and economic values stemming from such use of water and land.

Little effort has been made since CCC days to modify the second practice (the high-cost design and construction of local engineering works). Some negative effects of this practice have been discussed under "Public Facilities Planning" in the preceding subsection. These effects will intensify as contract construction prices, based on urban cost levels, continue to rise.

Education — The comments under this same heading in the preceding section on appropriate regional industrial development apply equally forcibly to agricultural technique. While it is true that some educational resources are directed toward small-holding agronomy (particularly on the part of the Extension Service), the effort falls far short of the task, if we contemplate a thoroughgoing revision of agricultural practice in the direction of higher skill, greater diversity, and intensive specialization. The total Extension staff engaged in informational and educational work in the uplands is a negligible percentage of the non-urban population. Of the two major State institutions of learning in the uplands, the larger (Highlands University) is frankly dedicated to achievement in the realm of physics and the most sophisticated sciences as well as conventional teacher training. (Geographically, it is also located at best peripherally to the region.) The other smaller but centrally located institution — the Northern New Mexico State School — operates on the vocational level and concentrates on such subjects as cosmetology, barbering, secretarial training, nurse-aide training, and auto mechanics. According to a recent resolution presented by its Board of Regents to the Constitutional Convention, its avowed purpose is to "help young villagers break away from their timid environment and to help them gain the confidence that they need to work in larger centers."* The one agricultural experiment station allotted to the uplands is located in the abundantly watered Espanola Valley near a principal commercial town and

* **Rio Grande Sun,** Espanola, October 2, 1969, news story.

55

at the lowest altitude to be encountered in the region. A far denser network of smaller research and demonstration units would be desirable, closely integrated with typical village communities of the various climatic and resources sub-areas of the region.

Public facilities planning — A denser network of intra-regional paved "tertiary" roads, as discussed under this same heading in the preceding section, would probably benefit local specialty agriculture and associated food industries by facilitating convenient, low-cost, small-lot distribution throughout the region. More specifically, a system of village-based *mercados,* with cold storage and other food processing and handling equipment, would further facilitate this type of economic development. At present such institutions are not included in the usual repertory of community or publicly sponsored facilities, although they are so classed in many parts of the world. They are also embedded in both the Spanish and the "Anglo" traditions, as witness the important role public farmers' and produce markets played in the development of the original New England and Atlantic Coast settlements and still play throughout Latin America.

The entrepreneurial environment — This socioeconomic factor probably affects the evolution of specialty regional agriculture only indirectly, in the degree to which it complicates the establishment and management of any type of local business or industry, whether on a private or cooperative basis. The considerations here are much the same as those discussed in the preceding section under the same heading.

Community modes of organization — Social and administrative arrangements tending to focus and intensify local community social and economic interaction should increase opportunities for regional agricultural specialization and trade. Markets maintained by village or other local organizations could play an especially useful role in this process.

56

Technical and agricultural research — Previous remarks on the scarcity of research in the United States on small-scale production techniques are fully applicable to agriculture. Most of the current "solutions" to the "farm problem" consist of recommendations in one form or another for the consolidation of small farming operations and the disposal of their output in bulk on the commercial market so that accepted large-scale machinery and methods may be used. The alternative and more realistic solution for a region such as the uplands — to refine and improve family- and village-scaled production geared to the local economy — needs far more serious attention.

POTENTIAL III: Deep and functional community involvement in soil and biotic conservation.

Customary usage — "Conservation," as a formally conceived policy or goal, dates to the early decades of this century, notably the Theodore Roosevelt-Gifford Pinchot era. It came into existence primarily as a reaction against the massive damage done to land and forests throughout the West by the ruthless commercial timbering and grazing practices of the preceding several decades. That such damage did not occur during the early period of provincial and colonial occupation was probably not due to a conscious tradition of conservation amongst the Hispanic settlers, as whole provinces in the Spain from which they emigrated had been devastated by overgrazing as early as the latter Middle Ages. It was due, rather, to the relatively small scale of the agricultural and pastoral husbandry of these earlier New World communities which almost automatically maintained a reasonable balance with the natural restorative powers of the land. (Nevertheless, localized instances of overgrazing, especially by sheep and goats, and of ill-judged land clearance by fire did occur. Additionally, cultivated village lands of the Santa Fé Formation also suffered damage from over-use, due to their fragile and erodable nature.)

The liberal Anglo-American policy of agency-administered "conservation" programs and regulations received great impetus in New Mexico under the New Deal in the 1930s, as outlined in Part One. Since then, these policies have been, to the extent feasible, built into the routine duties of

57

several Federal agencies. The most active of these is, of course, the Soil Conservation Service which operates presently in the uplands region through ten Soil and Water Conservation Districts embracing over 8 million acres of land, administered by a permanent and part-time technical and professional staff of 27 persons. Supplementing the activities of this organization, the Forest Service applies conservation management principles to the lands under its control to the extent possible under budgetary limitations, rising labor costs, and the demands for commercial timber harvesting. The Bureau of Land Management, through Grazing Districts functioning in the region, also attempts to encourage conservation practices such as grazing restriction and cooperative range management. The total manpower engaged in such efforts within the region now represents a very small percentage of the regional labor force and is far below the peak reached during the New Deal heyday.

Nevertheless, these programs have checked the extreme destruction characteristic of the earlier commercial exploitation of New Mexico range and wildlands and have partially restored some of the ravaged terrains.

The point to be made here is that these routine agency practices, adequate for the past several decades of transition, are probably inappropriate to handle the growing environmental and population pressures we face, and the necessity for a considerably enhanced comprehensive ecological management of wildlands including in its goals the wellbeing of their associated human community. This will probably involve much greater participation of that community at proportionately higher levels of skill and motivation.

" . . . The question arises, what is the ultimate magnitude of the enterprise of government conservation?" asks Aldo Leopold, one of America's leading geographer-ecologists. "Will the tax base carry its eventual ramifications? At what point will government conservation, like the mastodon, become handicapped by its own dimensions? The answer, if there is any, seems to be in a land ethic, or some other force which assigns more obligation to the private landowner."*

* **"A Sand County Almanac,"** Oxford University Press, 1949.

The intensification of productive economic life in northern New Mexico leading towards far more complete, more enlightened, and more rewarding participation of the people and communities of this region in the conservative and restorative management of its native resources would seem to be a most logical and applicable answer to this query.

Land and resources management (governmental) — Acknowledging the difficulties inherent in any attempt to evaluate government resources-management policies in relation to conservation from the point of view of this study, it is nevertheless reasonable to point out that most public agencies have been subject to the same pressure of rising labor costs as has private industry, forcing a trend toward mechanization along with increasing complication and size of operations. The inevitable result has been decreasing reliance on deployment of manpower in conservation works of all sorts and its replacement by conservation practices which may be carried out as largely as possible by power machinery. Such practices are particularly evident in the substitution of various types of metering, desilting, and detention dams, and of levees and channel rectification for flood management in place of comprehensive watershed and basin treatment programs. The latter approach would involve wide use of manpower in vegetative management, small check dams and water-spreading structures, soil treatment for increase of infiltration, etc., etc. The gigantic projects of the Corps of Engineers and the Bureau of Reclamation epitomize this manpower-eliminating tendency. But even the Soil Conservation Service, in its "watershed protection" policies, now relies more heavily on relatively large contractor-built retardation dams and levees for its protective measures than on labor-intensive land, soil, and vegetative treatment.

Similar trends may be noted in the modern Forest Service practice of silviculture which attempts to achieve conservation ends by such devices as the regulation of the timing, spacing, and procedures of large mechanized timbering operations; by segregating sectors of forest to limited uses; by blanket rationing of stock grazing; by airborne pesticide or herbicide applications, fire patrols, and vegetation surveys; by the mass chaining and bulldozing of brush and scrub terrains. Useful and necessary though these

59

devices may be under certain conditions, there is evidence that they can never achieve the sophisticated level of forest health, landscape improvement, multiple-use productivity, and aesthetic appeal which intensive on-the-ground fieldwork by skilled forest technicians can achieve. Similarly, in the sphere of hydrologic regimen modification, the tremendous importance of basin-wide practices designed to improve water retention and infiltration, and resulting soil moisture and subsurface storage and water quality is being increasingly recognized by scientists as a more effective answer to water management needs of the future than the continued construction of large dams with their heavy evaporation losses, adverse upstream effect on riverbed aggradation, and loss of capacity by siltation. In 1951, for example, the National Water Policy Board of the Engineers' Joint Council endorsed the concept of underground water storage as preferable to surface storage wherever practicable. "It is safe to say that during the next fifty years, the science of such storage will become one of the most important factors in the national water policy." *

Generally speaking, the present reliance on mechanized and "bureaucratized" conservation practices results from well-intentioned attempts to maximize, in the face of ever-mounting labor costs, the results achieved within the limitations of agency budgets. Such a rationale may be approaching the end of its usefulness. Very serious consideration should be given to the alternative philosophy of optimizing the total productivity of wildlands and forests through involving the regional community in a "vertically integrated" complex of land, environmental, and biotic-resource industries. Through such involvement, subsistence- and income-generation within the region may be increased very substantially and the regional economy may support and justify a far greater labor- and skill-intensive employment in the entire gamut of conservation work than it can at present. Public land and water management policies shaped toward this end should become the object of intensive research efforts.

* **"Big Dam Foolishness, The Problem of Modern Flood Control and Water Storage,"** E.T. Peterson, The Devin-Adair Company, New York, 1954.

Education — It is obvious that, should a general movement towards greater social and community involvement in comprehensive conservation management of native resources be realized in the uplands, such a movement should both justify and be facilitated by far more complete education and training in this and related fields. Both the increasing volume of employment and career opportunities in this type of work and the increasing sophistication and specialization in its various aspects would warrant such a commitment. Education of this kind could begin with introductory courses in the regular curricula of public elementary and high schools (as has been repeatedly proposed by the former New Mexico Conservation Education Association and other groups and endorsed by educators). Advanced vocational training could be offered in schools such as the Northern New Mexico State School. (See the related discussion of this possibility under Potential II.) A Youth Land Corps institute could ideally integrate comprehensive training in conservation and ecological management skills with field work in connection with vocational training and similar programs authorized through a number of anti-poverty and economic development agencies. A program of this kind could take in a wide variety of subjects at the technical aide and field work level such as: plane and topographic surveying; drafting and cartography; soil science and soil classification; plant classification and ecological mapping; elementary ecology; geology and landform analysis; climatology and hydrology; agronomy, range, and farm management; wildlife and recreational management and planning; silviculture; erosion control; revegetation; waterflow and watershed management; landscape architecture; field engineering (hydraulic, road, construction); economic and cultural geography.

An educational program of this kind could open horizons of opportunity to a substantial portion of New Mexico youth by:

1. familiarizing them with their environment in a new and richer perspective which would help them visualize and grasp a far wider range of opportunities at hand; and

2. preparing them for specific careers and employment opportunities throughout the nation and, in fact, the world, as resource-management programs in developing nations (and, hopefully, the United States) grow more sophisticated and intensive.

Public facilities planning — Dams and related water-control structures comprise the type of public facility with the most obvious and direct bearing on conservation practice. As discussed in other parts of this study, a trend away from the massive "main-stem-dam-and-levee" formula of river control and towards the upstream multiple-small-dam-and-watershed-management technique would greatly benefit the regional ecology and would release important public funds for use in effective land treatment and conservation work. Numerous small dams could be planned in close integration with community water supply and recreational needs and could be operated in conjunction with a wide range of runoff-retardation, erosion control, and aquifer recharging practices. ". . . Water resources in the mountain valleys can be developed so as to give better distribution of water over time by a) increasing the retention of snow and infiltration of rain and snowmelt by control of vegetation and land terracing; b) constructing small ponds and contour furrows to store or recharge surface runoff; and c) drilling wells to recover recharged ground water," writes one of New Mexico's foremost authorities on basin hydrology. * He continues, "The first two methods can be applied best in conjunction with a general program of watershed rehabilitation and development for recreation that is designed to use hand labor in thinning surplus trees and scrub growth, planting more useful tree species, constructing well-designed trails, roads, and associated runoff detention structures. Effective use of mountain forests requires dispersion of the users into small camp, picnic, and fishing areas that blend into the natural beauty of the area. A well-designed program of recreation development should also provide for education in water and forest conservation techniques."

Highway planning and design offer another good means of relating public facilities to conservation. Although progress has been made in recent years, much remains to be done in revamping the location, runoff arrangements, and planning of roads so that they may act as stabilizing and restoring agencies in the landscape rather than as pathways of aggravated erosion.

*   Dr. Zane Spiegel, unpublished communication, February 1963.

The entrepreneurial environment — Fiscal and legal policies affecting conservation activity would include such devices as tax rebate incentives to encourage conservation practices on private lands and more effective laws enforcing such practices where damage to downstream or adjacent properties, the general hydrologic regimen, wildlife and vegetation, water quality, etc., result. Legal devices such as the special purpose easement, secured by purchase or the exercise of eminent domain for such purposes as scenic or watershed protection, could also fall into this category of policies. This is a complex and difficult subject involving questions of equity and demanding administration of very high caliber. Not much progress can be hoped for until the general public becomes much more aware of the "land ethic" imperative. Nevertheless, it should be mentioned here as warranting intensive study.

Community modes of organization — Many conservation practices, particularly those concerned with watershed regimen improvement, require comprehensive planning and execution over a complete drainage system. Close cooperation between public land custodial agencies and numerous private landowners is usually necessary for programs of this kind. Effective local community organization would greatly facilitate such cooperation, especially if the same organization provided the medium through which local people could work toward improved multiple use and management of the full range of natural resources of the area. The present soil and water conservation district tends to be too large and diffuse to achieve this localized focusing of community interests. Conservancy and irrigation districts, the alternative vehicle for local action on water management, are, by tradition and mandate, very limited in their permitted range of activities. As formal branches of State government with taxing powers, they are often difficult to set up because of local fear of involvement in political and fiscal problems. There may be a need for some type of innovative resources development district comprising a logical and functional hydrologic area system supporting a group of village communities closely enough linked to have common economic interests and social ties. The "sub-basin" or "microbasin" has been proposed as the geographic basis of such a district for ecologic and economic development planning and action. *

Technical and agricultural research — The opinion may be hazarded here that conservation is one field in which technical knowledge of methods and potentials considerably outruns application. Examples of benefits obtained by various controlled experiments in pilot watersheds, range areas, forest districts, ranches, and farms are legion in the literature. What is lacking is the continuous, intensive, and widespread application of this knowledge. It might be mentioned, however, that the type of deep community involvement in conservation practice and ecological management discussed in this section would provide abundant manpower and opportunity for continued and creative field research in relevant techniques.

POTENTIAL IV: **Enrichment of village community economic, social, and cultural life.**

Customary usage — There are very few regions within the United States where the small land-rooted village maintains its hold in the physical and cultural landscape as strongly as in the New Mexico uplands — and this despite several generations of adverse economic influences. This circumstance is doubtless due to a combination of factors, amongst them:

1. The "land logic" of a semiarid mountainous terrain within which human settlement naturally gravitates to watershed valleys where small-scale irrigation subsistence agriculture is feasible, yet where access to surrounding forests and high pastures is convenient.

2. The isolation of the entire region from the main metropolitan and industrial centers of the continent and its colonization during a period of

* See **"Water and Related Land Resources Survey, Upper Rio Grande Basin,"** U.S. Department of Agriculture and New Mexico State Engineer, 1969; also see **"Development Potentials of the Northern New Mexico Uplands,"** Peter van Dresser, 1962.

handicraft industry and non-mechanized transportation technology.

3. The conservatism and social cohesion of the settlers derived from a long heritage of similar village-centered life in the old world, from powerful ties of kinship, and from a deep shared religious tradition.

As a result of such factors, the uplands villages functioned for generations as "micro-urban" centers for religious dispensation, for elementary government administration, for mutual protection, for the practice of simple craft and trade specializations (blacksmithing, cartwrighting, harness-making, grist-milling, etc.), for commerce and barter, and for social and festive gatherings. One of the most distinctive architectural styles in the United States evolved out of these functions and a life-style which still molds strongly the sentiments of tens of thousands of regional dwellers of all ages.

The long drawn-out decline of this village culture is evident in the many abandoned houses, churches, and schools, in unmaintained *acequias* and fields, in ruined grist mills, and deserted hamlets. Village *fiestas* and *bailes* are still attended, but the mechanized carnival, the juke box, and easy access by television or car to commerical entertainment robs them of the color and vitality of an earlier period. The essential question arises: Is this decline inevitable in the march towards "modernity," and hence to be deplored solely for sentimental and "romantic" reasons? Or is it an indication of a failure of our general society (to its own detriment) to recognize, adapt to, and build upon permanent values in this regional life-style?

Land and resources management (governmental) — Little direct influence of public land and resources agencies on village life is apparent. Yet, indirectly, this influence is strong and usually detrimental. The unavoidable necessities of bureaucratic administration by which policy decisions are made in central offices and carried out by subordinates in the field places local communities in a passive role as regards the use and management of most of the lands and other native resources around them. This lack of a meaningful decision-making function inevitably contributes to the lowered morale and social disintegration of village communities.

Many resources agencies have attempted to counter this effect through setting up various types of area advisory committees, with locally elected members (e.g., Soil and Water Conservation District Boards, Grazing District Committees, Highway Planning Committees). Such bodies tend to become at best interpreters of pre-set directives and at worst "rubber stamps" for the decisions of paid technical and professional functionaries of the agencies involved. They are seldom capable of launching bold programs which would capture the imagination and enthusiasm of local communities.

Serious efforts should be made to replace this type of token democracy with increasingly meaningful participation of local communities in the conservative management and profitable use of the surrounding environmental resources. Such a policy is admittedly very difficult to carry out. Much must be done to cultivate local leadership and technical ability competent to assume new responsibilities and avoid mistakes of the past. There will also be required a reorientation in much standard bureaucratic thinking. Policies will have to become more adaptable, lines of command more flexible. Technical staffs and planning offices will have to be decentralized and set up in local centers for maximum involvement in community life and the local decision-making process. Professional people selected for this work and residence should be chosen for their ability to work effectively with local people; their insight and judgment as to ways and means through which people can economically use and manage natural resources and their proficiency in resolving on-the-spot problems.

These are stringent requirements. Yet, if we hope to achieve the high level of intelligent utilization of the natural resources of the region which the future demands, some such enlargement of public policy seems essential. In its course, opportunities for satisfying and creative careers within the villages must increase and, with them, the vitality of individual and community life.

Education — The detrimental effects of current educational policies on village life have been discussed in several sub-sections of this study. These may be summarized briefly here:

1. The physical closing of schools in numerous villages has an extremely damaging effect on community morale. Such closings are routinely justified on budgetary and efficiency grounds and are built into both State- and

Federal-aid educational policy. Yet virtually no effort has been made to assess the cumulative socioeconomic effects of this policy on the regional community, nor its real costs to the State in terms of accelerated population erosion and economic decline. A new look needs to be taken at school consolidation as the universal cure-all for educational problems. Studies such as the "Catskill Area Project" suggest that small schools can be vital institutions,* and it is probable that more public expenditures are justified for their maintenance and improvement than a narrow bookkeeping analysis indicates.

2. The increasing use of pre-fab school buildings built by urban contracting firms (and usually located away from the centers of villages) tends to rob the local communities of a sense of participation in the educational process and deprives them of an important life-reinforcing activity which should be taking place in the physical core of the community. The architectural character of such buildings (assembled of extruded metal and plastic, windowless, etc.) amounts to a deliberate denial of the regional cultural heritage and helps alienate the children from a sense of continuity with the best in their own tradition.

3. The persistent orientation of most curricula towards indoctrination in urban values and towards preparation for urban careers further adds to this alienation. Realistic appraisal of conditions in metropolitan areas does not justify this exclusive orientation.

Public facilities planning — Very little true "public facilities planning" is done in relation to the uplands villages. This is, no doubt, due to the general economic and population stasis in most of them, to the conservatism of the residents, and to the lack of municipal corporations or other organizations to sponsor such projects. The most common public facilities encountered are, of course, schools, churches, *acequia* systems, roads, domestic water systems, and post offices. All of these facilities, to the extent that they are "planned" at all, are handled by mutually independent

* See **"Rural Renaissance: Revitalizing Small High Schools,"** U.S. Department of Health, Education, and Welfare, 1961; also **"Multiple Classes: Learning in Small Groups."**

commissions or agencies, most of which meet only sporadically. There is usually complete lack of coordination between them and almost no familiarity with the goals and concepts of town or village planning. As a result, no cumulative development of village architecture or civic character occurs such as might be attained through sensible site and circulation planning and grouping of buildings and other facilities to form something resembling a community center or plaza (this, despite the early traditions to this effect under Spanish colonial administration).

A general enlargement of social and economic life in the uplands should certainly be complemented by progress in village design and community facilities planning. Such design and planning should reinterpret the best of the regional village heritage in terms of the requirements and amenities of the future. "We must work out new forms to meet new needs and to use new possibilities," writes one of England's foremost authorities on village and town planning.* "But this does not mean that we should ignore the achievements of the past. . . A study of the principles of design, whether they were conscious or unconscious, which have given our English villages their beauty, their charm, and their character, may well elucidate principles that will be useful in our new building." This admonition applies with full force to the unique communities of the New Mexico uplands although, at this writing, it is difficult to specify from what sources and through what channels the necessary talents and architectural sensitivity may be brought to bear on the problem.**

The entrepreneurial environment — The effects on village development of this group of social and economic influences are generally

* **"The Anatomy of a Village,"** by Thomas Sharp, Harmondsworth, 1946.

** Since this was written, the Center for Environmental Studies at the University of New Mexico has published a proposal for the architectural and town-planning study of four villages in the Manzanares Mountains, looking towards their rehabilitation as satellite communities in the Albuquerque region.

68

indirect and have been discussed in several preceding subsections. In brief, to the extent that our present "entrepreneurial environment" favors large-scaled more centralized and more highly capitalized businesses over smaller-scaled and localized enterprises, to that same extent profitable and productive activities in local communities are handicapped. It is obvious that this handicap depresses the quality of village life. In rural England and Western Europe, for example, villages with populations of 350 or less commonly house six or eight types of stores, workshops, and inns which cater to local needs and contribute greatly to the vitality and interest of the community. In the uplands, villages of this size at best support a meager general store and bar. As part of any general program of regional regeneration, all factors contributing to this deficiency should be studied and modified to the extent possible.

Community modes of organization — Lack of institutions and organizational channels for community and group achievement, also discussed in several preceding sub-sections, obviously and seriously blocks opportunities for the establishment of a whole range of social, civil, and economic services and activities in village communities. It has been pointed out that the earlier cultural heritage of the original settlers provided for such community institutions and organizations and competent studies should be undertaken to learn how these traditions may be revitalized and reinterpreted to meet future needs.

Technical and agricultural research — Relocation and reorientation of various research programs to meet the challenges of small-scale industry and specialty agriculture could obviously bring new and vital activities into villages and their vicinities. A whole new range of "mini-stations" for agricultural and agrestal field studies should be established throughout the region, and their staffs should be selected for commitment to rural redevelopment and should be stationed permanently in these decentralized stations. Close and continuous collaboration should, of course, be carried out with local people. Similar projects in village-based industries would further add to the meaningful activity at the local level.

PART THREE
A PHYSIOGRAPHIC BASIS FOR DEVELOPMENT CONCEPTS

PART THREE

A PHYSIOGRAPHIC BASIS FOR DEVELOPMENT CONCEPTS

The Present Geographical Patterns

A holistic overview of the physical and cultural determinants of life in the uplands, such as we have attempted in Parts One and Two of this study, can lead to some useful unifying concepts to guide planning and economic development efforts in the region along ecologic lines. Part Three will sketch some such concepts which have occurred to the author.

We may begin by roughly organizing our statistical and quantitative knowledge of the region along geographic lines. Fig. 5 is a simple political or cultural map of the uplands as they exist in this decade. The heavy dashed line represents the approximate boundaries of the region as determined from the various physiographic characteristics discussed in Part One. The preponderant dotted areas or tracts running up and down the eastern and western lobes of the region are National Forest lands. The smaller cross-hatched tracts are Indian reservations, all of the Pueblo type — considerably smaller than the large reservations typical of the Plains Indian groups in the lower and more arid parts of the State. I have also sketched the outline of three embryo "urbanizing" or "sub-metropolitan" zones within the region (heavy dotted lines). The largest of these is the Santa Fe-Espanola-Los Alamos triad in the lower center. This is the locale of the most active

73

modernization connected with Federal scientific installations, State government expansion, tourism, and commercial agriculture. Smaller zones of urbanization, mostly associated with tourism, occur around the old pueblo metropolis and Spanish trading town of Taos, in the northeast, and around Las Vegas, built up during the first heyday of rail communications with the East when the town was a main terminus and cattle market.

The principal vital and economic indices of this region, as of 1960, stood somewhat as follows:

Population: 133,000 (14% of the State total) or about 10 per square mile. Fifty-one percent of this population was classified as urban (State average, 65%). The balance, although called "rural" by the Census Bureau, lived, as before suggested, mostly in small hamlets and villages, not on isolated farms, as the term implies in much of the United States. These settlements were above the national average in proportion of children, and below in proportion of younger adults. As a whole, the population has remained constant since 1940, although certain of the more remote sectors, as villages on the lower eastern and southeastern piedmonts of the Sangre de Cristos, have suffered severe losses which have only been compensated within the region by growth of certain towns, subject to the newer urbanizing forces, especially Santa Fé and the Espanola valley. Even so, the population density of the region in 1960 was 40% higher than that of the State as a whole, despite the rapid growth of a few new-era cities outside the region.

"Basic" or "primary" economic activity of the region may be estimated for 1960 at about $70 or $80 million. The largest single component of this income-generating activity was about $30 million of funds funneled into the region from outside (although these dollars, of course, do not represent "production" in the pure sense). Probably over half of this flow was in payment for the exported labor of private residents working as far away as California, Montana, or Michigan. Somewhat less than half represents government net payments, either in the form of welfare subsidies

74

Figure 5

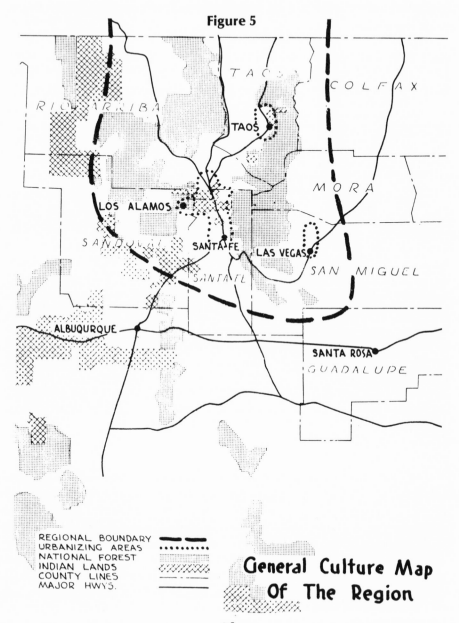

REGIONAL BOUNDARY ▬ ▬ ▬
URBANIZING AREAS ••••••••••
NATIONAL FOREST
INDIAN LANDS
COUNTY LINES
MAJOR HWYS. ——————

General Culture Map
Of The Region

75

or wages for government employment.

The next largest primary productive activity was the growing of *livestock and crops* which yielded a census-recorded value of about $17 million. This figure reflected a rather low average dollar value per agricultural acre — $25-$35 for irrigated croplands, $2 for grazed lands. The relative size of the total expresses the still dominant agricultural preoccupation of the people, while the low unit value indicates the strongly subsistence orientation of that preoccupation. Fig. 6, prepared by the U.S. Agricultural Research Service, depicts graphically this subsistence pattern of farming in the northcentral counties, as indicated by average size of farms in 1950.

Primary funds released by *travelers and tourists* in search of recreation are difficult to estimate, but the best data I have been able to gather suggests a total annual value of about $16 million for 1960.

Forest-product yield, which a superficial look at the geography of the region would suggest as one of the major sources of revenue, probably averaged about $7 million total value annually for 1960 and a number of preceding years. Figure 4 (page 13) depicts the area of commercial timber stands of the northcentral counties in the mid-1950s, as calculated by the State Department of Economic Development. The somewhat less than 5,000 square miles of such timberlands shown here averaged a yield of about $1,400 per square mile, and probably not over 1,200 to 1,500 of the total labor force of 30,000 were employed in forest care, timber harvesting, and wood-products manufacturing.

Other miscellaneous manufacturing produced a greater value-added than the forest-based activity — probably around $8 million. The percentage of people so employed was, surprisingly enough, not very different from the State average. The bulk of such activity was concentrated in Santa Fé.

Mining, although for long a colorful component of the regional

76

landscape, produced a total value of something like $2 million, if one aggregates the output of the several small coal, mica, beryl, etc., workings scattered throughout the mountains.

Productivity and the Rural Syndrome

The total of these "primary" revenues, complemented by a slightly smaller total of "secondary" activities in trade, services, utilities, construction, finance, etc., stood at about $130 million, which represents a per capita income of somewhat under $1,000 in this region, compared with a State average of about $1,900.

Evaluated in terms of productivity reduced to a land area basis, the total yield of the region in values derived from land resources may be estimated for this period at about $4.70 per acre, or about $3,000 per square mile.

In common with the statistics for most highland and hinterland regions of the United States, these figures suggest the presence of the classic syndrome — discussed in Part One — of rural economic depression and population stagnation in the northern New Mexico uplands, outside of the small nodes of urbanization. Bypassed by the march of progress, isolated from mass markets, situated amidst rugged terrains unsuitable for large-scale agriculture or large-scale timber cropping, the traditionally self-contained regional economy has tended to falter. Fields and *acequias* in numerous valleys have been neglected and dwellings abandoned. Young people have emigrated to the cities in search of employment and wider horizons.

The infiltration of certain benefits from the general progress of society and the nationwide technological advance — such as paved roads, rural electrification, and modern school buildings; the welfare and custodial programs of various Federal and State agencies; the penetration of some tourist trade — have not sufficed to counteract these competitive disadvantages in the modern world and the region, outside its principal urbanizing core, continues to lose relatively in economic and population status, and perhaps even absolutely in the latter. Extrapolated a few more decades, this trend has been interpreted by many to imply an ultimate complete decay and disappearance of the traditional culture and economy.

Despite this generally negative prognosis and current fascination

77

Figure 6

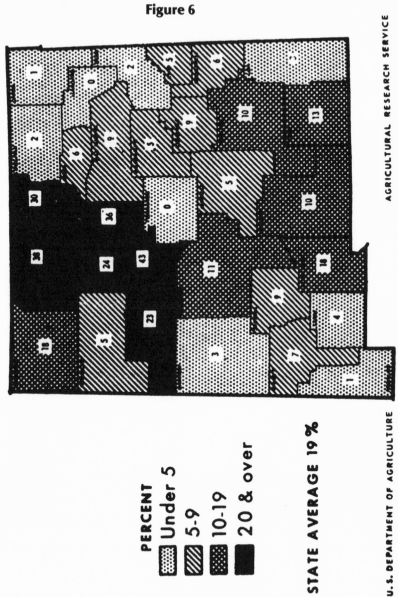

FARMS UNDER 10 ACRES
New Mexico, 1950

PERCENT
Under 5
5-9
10-19
20 & over

STATE AVERAGE 19%

AGRICULTURAL RESEARCH SERVICE

U.S. DEPARTMENT OF AGRICULTURE

78

exerted by booming metropolitan centers and retirement and research complexes, the destiny of this regional community continues to be of considerable general concern. To a large extent this is a reflection of the unique cultural heritage embodied here, and of the stubborn vitality of this tradition under adverse circumstances.

But this factor is reinforced by the physiographically determined role of the region as an important water catchment area in a chronically thirsty territory. With each passing decade, the strategic importance of this function becomes more sharply emphasized. The large irrigation districts and dams established during the first half of the 20th century along the lower reaches of the three major rivers, the more recent missile-age defense establishments planted about the State, the booming metropolitan resort-retirement housing developments constitute powerful and water-hungry new elements in the body politic whose needs must be responded to.

Simultaneously, the mounting national demand for outdoor recreational *lebensraum* in an era of restless rubber-tired tourism focuses a parallel attention on the naturally verdant wildlands and forests and the scenic vistas of the higher portions of this mountain enclave. The question of the future optimum management, control, and exploitation of such lands, and of the life-giving waters which they command, thus becomes increasingly insistent, and has for some time been spurring various reactions in the fields of government administration, planning, and entrepreneurial activity, not to speak of politics.

Until very recently, the general drift of these reactions, insofar as concepts of economic development and resources management for this region are concerned, has been dominated by contemporary theory in the fields of industrial analysis, investment management, and economic planning — especially as this practice has crystallized since World War II. The prescriptions of this policy — which one encounters at many levels and in many functional divisions of government, in academic circles, and in the councils of business and finance — are by now virtually codified into a body of economic development procedure for "emerging societies." This procedure calls for the formation of an "infrastructure" of basic public facilities — usually multimillion-dollar dams and canals, power networks, and heavy-duty highways. In recreational areas which are, or can be made, accessible to a mass public, this infrastructure may also include

79

governmentally improved scenic parks and preserves in particularly favored sites. This sector of public deficit-financed construction is, in turn, intended to facilitate the channeling of large-scale private (usually corporate) investment into such income-generating, export-oriented projects as bulk wood-processing plants, deluxe resort complexes, irrigated monocultural plantations, or consolidated ranching operations.

Examples of most of these prescriptions for economic advancement are to be found in various stages of projection or completion by a variety of agencies and interests throughout or adjacent to the northern New Mexico uplands.

Applied in a thoroughgoing fashion, *this policy might be described as one of orderly evacuation of the region*, followed or accompanied by a planned reconstruction of its economy in terms of the large-scale rationalized and mechanized installations capable of competitive survival in the age of automation. Complementing this technological reconstruction, there is visualized the extension and intensification of custodial management by appropriate agencies, of wildland preserves — for recreation, for water yield, for limited forest production, for carefully restricted livestock grazing, and for wilderness values. A reduction in permanent population is implicitly accepted as perhaps an inevitable byproduct of this economic overhauling, since the remaining population may the more readily be retrained to the technical skills appropriate to the limited, but higher paying, employment requirements of the new-era operations.

Despite the impression of rigorous logical necessity conveyed by this doctrine of economic development, and despite its wide acceptance and often authoritative presentation, I think it necessary that we keep in mind certain of its inherent limitations and drawbacks, particularly in relation to physiocultural regions of the kind we are considering here.

The most serious of these drawbacks arises from the fact that a very large proportion — probably the bulk — of the economic benefits and the potentials for resources improvement associated with such a region are of the kind which can only be realized by a labor-, skill-, and people-intensive pattern of land use and productive organization, rather than by the machine-, capital-, and system-intensive operations of contemporary development theory.

Amongst the benefits and potentials so realizable must be included practically the entire range of improvements in biotic yields (forests, stock, game), soil condition, recreational opportunity, and even hydraulic management. All these useful fields of endeavor, while strikingly responsive to the application of scientific knowledge, are dependent on the continuous deployment of intelligent and dedicated human effort over extensive land areas in essentially personal and manual tasks. This is especially true in a region of rugged terrain, pocketed and mixed timber stands and vegetative types, easily erodable soil, and marginal precipitation.

By its inherent nature, big technology operating through the big project (whether public or private) can realize only a fraction of these potentials. It must concentrate on those forms of resources-utilization or management which can be handled by machinery or equipment with the minimum of human involvement — the giant dam in the one strategic location, the deluxe lodge or marina at the choice scenic site, the super-highway through the most accessible valley-system, and the automated pulp or timber mill commanding the finest timber stands. Only by such tactics can it justify the investment it represents or compete with similar installations elsewhere. Frequently, despite such selective tactics, and with the most careful planning and engineering, it cannot so compete, and must be subsidized with the inevitable entrainment of bureaucratic and political complications.

In the course of this process of "development," this rationale usually accentuates and aggravates some of the most destructive tendencies of modern times. It recreates in provincial, rural, and primitive settings the very patterns of centralized congestion surrounded by sub-economic blight which is demoralizing our metropolitan areas. It reduces the cultural landscape to a sterile and institutional bleakness, punctuated by painfully artificial playgrounds and fun spots. It hastens the already unmanageable flow of displaced persons to our metropolitan slums, fringe areas, and economic ghettos, or to the shadow world of migratory labor. By maximizing the local dependance on national markets, on imported equipment and necessities, and on mass transportation, by failing to make use of whole sectors of local resources, it adds to the already enormous national drain on energy, strategic minerals, water, and even land. In short, examined in a broader frame of reference than that provided by the concept of "economics of scale" and by the calculus of investment, its claim to comprehensive efficiency and scientific validity is very dubious.

81

It is for such reasons that, in very recent years, an alternative philosophy of development, growing out of "ecologic" considerations, has attracted increasing interest. This philosophy suggests that the essential "infrastructure" for the uplands and for many other regions like it is not a system of giant dams and superhighways, but a thriving permanent population sustaining a way of life ecologically adapted to the regional environment. It suggests that this way of life must be essentially "bioeconomic," that is, dependent on the skillful utilization of primarily biological flow-resources and on close adaptation of logistic arrangements and productive facilities to the regional topography and biotic patterns, rather than on high-energy machine technology and large-scale commerce.

It suggests that the place-rooted community, with access to an adequate geographical base, and embracing within its membership a considerable range of differentiated and complementary human skills, is the normal and efficient embodiment of these principles. It suggests that real capital formation in communities of this kind can proceed effectively without the accumulation of debt, through the application of self-directed labor to cost-free indigenous materials, and that this process can lead to a wide diffusion of small-scale productive installations which can aggregate to impressive totals and can result in a highly evolved cultural and economic landscape. It suggests that it is this pattern of "bioeconomic" growth which must be facilitated in the uplands both because it offers the only efficient type of human use of such a region and because it offers our best hope of solving the problems of resources-management and conservation which press upon us with the increasing maturity of our society.

A Matrix for Future Growth

An overview of the physiographic pattern of life in this region, as before suggested, indicates that the existing traditional pattern of Hispanic settlement in the northern New Mexico uplands is a remarkably coherent expression of this principle of land use and economic organization — primitive and incomplete, no doubt, but uniquely suited for an evolutionary development towards the essential bioeconomic community of the future.

Through an apparent — but only an apparent — paradox, the very

82

aridity and ruggedness of the regional terrain has much to do with this favorable circumstance. In such an environment, the logic of topography and of hydrology strongly determines the conditions of human life. Here the watershed is no mere geographer's abstraction, but a microcosm to which social organization must quite specifically adapt itself. Its upper boundaries are usually steep and not conveniently crossed by roads; its drainage sump contains generally the only land suitable for settlement and intensive cultivation; and all social and economic activities of necessity ebb and flow through it. Additionally, the control and management of the water collected and sharply concentrated by gravity here imposes on the community an incentive for collective action internally, and a collective external responsibility to water users on the lower reaches of the stream system which the watershed feeds. Finally, the considerable range in elevation and climatic zones usually embraced within such a microcosm results in a corresponding range of biotic resources which encourages a healthy degree of internal differentiation in economic activities.

Fig. 7, traced from the Soil Conservation Service's map of small watersheds in New Mexico, indicates the intricate mosaic of such microcosms which compose the "uplands." Over 60 such units can be identified, averaging about 200 square miles each in surface area, and each containing usually at least one node of settlement. Fig. 8, reproduced from a study of the U.S. Agricultural Research Service, shows the fine-scaled subdivision of small holdings in the irrigated bottomland of one of the longest settled of these sites, that of Santa Cruz near the ancient first capital of the province. Note in the smaller scaled diagram at the lower center the small proportion this irrigated sector bears to the total watershed area. Fig. 9 depicts a larger drainage basin, that of the Puebla and Santa Barbara streams which discharge an annual 74,000 acre-feet of water into the Rio Grande at Embudo. This "microbasin," as it might be called, contains some seven or eight hamlets and villages (including one small pueblo) and supports a range of land uses from intensive orchards at the lower levels to hunting, skiing, and spruce timber harvesting at the higher.

As I have already suggested, most of these nodes of settlement should properly be regarded as urban microcosms, not mere haphazard collections of small farms. Over the centuries they have performed, on a miniature scale, many of the essential organizing functions for the regional economy. Within

83

them have been elaborated the techniques of building construction from indigenous materials (adobe, timber, caliche plaster), the simple but effective hydraulic engineering practices needful for local irrigation systems, the skills of food preparation and preserving, the crafts of blacksmithing, mill and wainwrighting, weaving, woodworking, tanning and harness-making, the institutional arrangement for the management of *ejidos* (communal grazing lands) and *acequias* (community irrigation ditches). Much of this knowledge was brought from similar mountain areas in the Spanish homeland. Some was adapted from Pueblo Indian practice. Some has vanished almost completely in recent decades. Some is still in daily use.

Ritual and sacrament combined to fortify the civic and communal awareness of each such urban microcosm. A patron saint watched over the fortunes of each, and *fiestas* and processions periodically celebrated this guardianship. Civil administration through the local *alcalde* and economic coordination through the *majordomo* and *patron* further reinforced this homogeneity.

A Pipe Dream

It would be a serious mistake to suppose that the march of technology has obsoleted the fundamental logic and the functional validity of the resulting pattern of land use. On the contrary, I believe this pattern offers a very remarkable potential for extension and for refinement to a high level of efficiency. Let me now ask your indulgence for a few moments of pipe-dreaming as to the possible results of such an extension and refinement.

Fig. 10 depicts in schematic form a typical uplands watershed community or microbasin as it exists in this decade (the left-hand figure in the diagram), and as it might evolve under an enlightened development philosophy (the right-hand figure). Note first that the focus or node of settlement — the traditional village shown at the forking of the principal stream (area 1 in the diagram) has not only retained but strengthened its strategic position over the quarter-century interval. It has not been flooded out by a high-level dam, gutted by a superhighway, or leveled for a commercial ranch site. Its population has, in fact, at least doubled, perhaps trebled. In short, it is continuing to serve as the essential, even if miniature, metropolis for the thriving economic and social life of the microbasin.

84

Figure 7

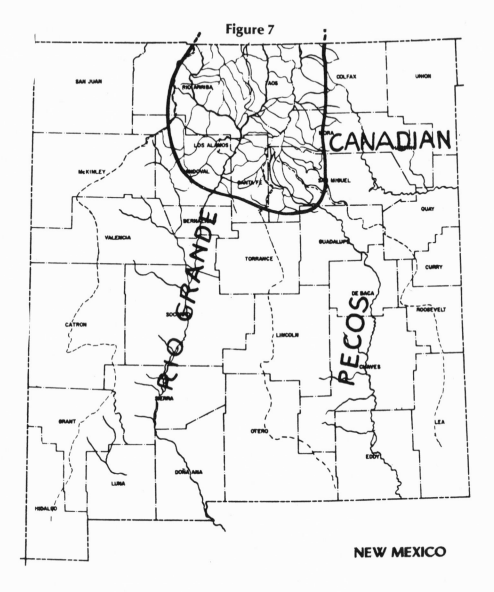

WATERSHED AND BASIN
DIVISIONS OF THE UPLANDS
PROVINCE.

Figure 8

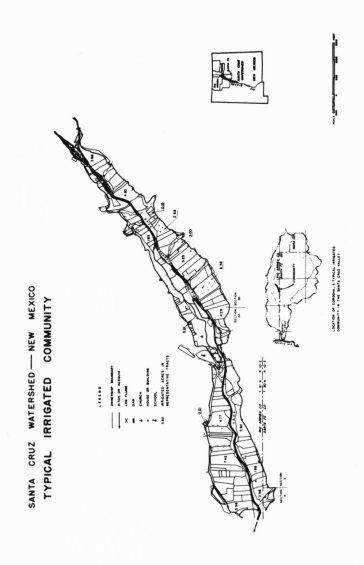

Figure 9

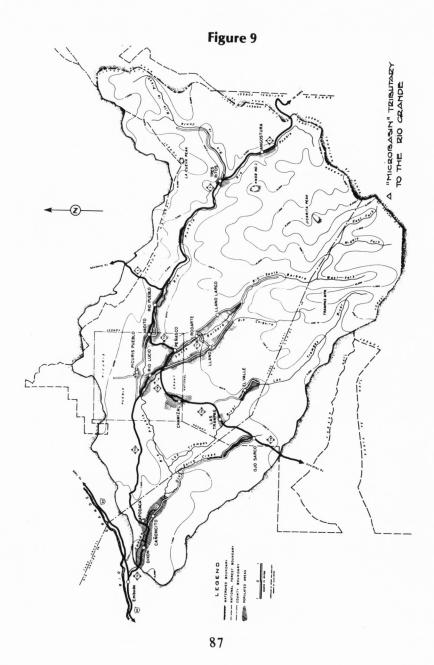

A "MICROBASIN" TRIBUTARY TO THE RIO GRANDE

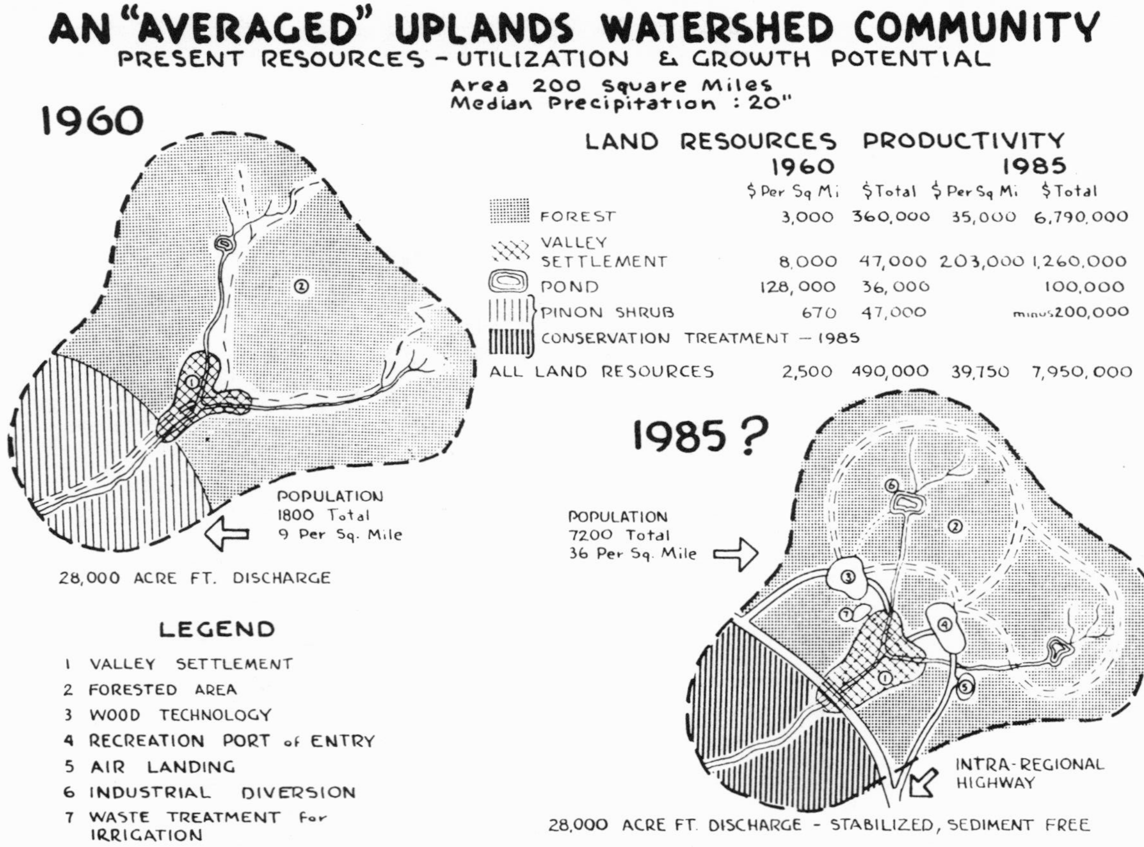

Figure 10

AN "AVERAGED" UPLANDS WATERSHED COMMUNITY

PRESENT RESOURCES - UTILIZATION & GROWTH POTENTIAL

Area 200 Square Miles
Median Precipitation : 20"

LAND RESOURCES PRODUCTIVITY

	1960		1985	
	$ Per Sq. Mi.	$ Total	$ Per Sq. Mi.	$ Total
FOREST	3,000	360,000	35,000	6,790,000
VALLEY SETTLEMENT	8,000	47,000	203,000	1,260,000
POND	128,000	36,000		100,000
PINON SHRUB	670	47,000		~200,000
CONSERVATION TREATMENT — 1985				
ALL LAND RESOURCES	2,500	490,000	39,750	7,950,000

1960

POPULATION
1800 Total
9 Per Sq. Mile

28,000 ACRE FT. DISCHARGE

1985 ?

POPULATION
7200 Total
36 Per Sq. Mile

INTRA-REGIONAL HIGHWAY

28,000 ACRE FT. DISCHARGE - STABILIZED, SEDIMENT FREE

LEGEND

1 VALLEY SETTLEMENT
2 FORESTED AREA
3 WOOD TECHNOLOGY
4 RECREATION PORT of ENTRY
5 AIR LANDING
6 INDUSTRIAL DIVERSION
7 WASTE TREATMENT for IRRIGATION

A new generation of skilled forest and rural technicians and their families live in this village and work almost continuously throughout the 200 square miles of the watershed lands. They are largely the sons and daughters of the present regional population who have benefited by challenging training and research programs carried on locally and who have a personal stake in the overall enterprise. As a result of this training, and of carefully worked-out agreements between government agencies, local landowners, and the local community, the entire watershed is now operated as an integrated ecologic system. Large sectors of second-growth, of insect- or fire-damaged forest inherited from previous generations have been brought to full yield and beauty through unprecedentedly intensive silvicultural practices. Vegetation management, extensive mulching, contour furrowing, and multiple check-dam construction have maximized soil moisture content, increased subsurface percolation and storage of water, and stabilized stream flows. Livestock has been considerably expanded but, by scientific deployment in relation to cover types and seasonal changes, has been kept a positive factor in the ecologic balance. An extensive complex of trails, camping sites, hostels, lodges, wells, and small dams designed by skilled landscape and park architects have been constructed and are in constant use by visitors from the lowlands. Moderate use-fees paid by these visitors defray the cost of supervision and maintenance of these facilities and add to local employment and community revenues.

Judicious site- and circulation-planning has channeled the "export" activities of the watershed community in harmony with this concept of organic and ecologic integrity. A good intraregional road touches the village and provides convenient access to the rest of the region and to major continental highways, but is deliberately routed away from scenic and settled valleys. A short spur connects this road with a recreational "port of entry" above the village (area 4) which provides good access to the forested highlands. Here campers and hikers may park their cars safely, hire horses if they wish, and enter the trail system. Perhaps there is even a small hovercraft field (area 5) for tourists arriving by private aircraft.

A similar spur connects to an industrial site (area 3) where any relatively large technical or industrial process may be carried out. These will depend on the characteristic biotic pattern of the watershed and the particular interests and entrepreneurial skills of local groups and the community. This site will

89

most probably contain at least an efficient and permanent sawmill of a capacity proportioned to the sustained yield output of the tributary forest zone. This may be supplemented by a number of byproducts-using installations — fence-post, pole, shingle, or molding mills, and the like. Fertilizers and mulches for local use may be produced here from bark and other wastes. Fuel, both solid and gaseous, sufficient for the entire watershed community, may also be a valuable byproduct. Other specialized production based on the adjacent biotic yield — as meatpacking, tanning, and woolscouring — may be carried on here at a relatively small but efficient scale for the domestic and regional market.

Processed water may be supplied to this site from an upstream impoundment (area 6), but after use it is clarified at a treatment lagoon (area 7) and re-used for irrigation of crops downstream.

Note that the great bulk of the capital improvements here sketched are the result of labor applied directly to easily available raw materials with simple tools. They can be achieved with a minimum of borrowing or outside investment. They consist of such things as trails, fences, corrals, small earth-and-rock dams, dug wells, log-and-stone buildings, land- and standing timber-treatment. Large-scale power machinery would be required only at a few points in the operations of this "bioeconomic" complex. Motorized equipment, for example, would be neither necessary nor desirable in the entire forest area. Sustained yield timber harvesting in a multiple-use setting could most effectively be carried on by an ancient and efficient invention (the draft horse), while the logistically efficient location of the sawmill and its auxiliaries reduce the transportation requirements to a minimum. The art of breeding and utilizing zoologic horsepower would be rediscovered and re-applied.

Similarly, recreational policy would be deliberately planned to satisfy the large and growing national demand for the selective personal wildlife experience, not dependent upon elaborate facilities.

The renaissance and restoration of the village itself would most directly embody this principle. The traditional architecture of adobe, timber, and stone would be strengthened and enriched, yet construction would remain on the largely do-it-yourself basis it has always been, and the home mortgage would be as rare a phenomenon as it was in 1970. The local *acequias* and the irrigated croplands of the village site would be improved by better layout, by

90

ditch lining, by terracing, and scientific soil conditioning, and would be largely converted to high-value vitamin and protein production for domestic consumption or the local market. But this would remain essentially a spare-time family and subsistence activity, not warranting the tractor and the big-field investment of commercial agriculture.

The village itself would no doubt also provide the setting for a variety of skill-intensive small-scale enterprises. These might include cottage and craft industries using indigenous raw materials as well as inns and summer places catering to travelers desiring interesting vacation destinations rather than one-night stopovers on main highways. No doubt specialized and advanced precision industries, on the Swiss pattern, would also find a suitable environment here. Finally, one would expect that local pride and initiative would lead to the embellishment of the village with such amenities as a library, a restored *plaza,* a *mercado,* a theater, perhaps a rodeo, sports, and fairground, and other civic adornments embedded in the Hispanic tradition and of perennial value and validity. It is hardly necessary to add that a strong public school, well oriented to the community, would be an indispensable local institution.

Our contemporary *hubris* of the big project and the mechanized mass operation makes it extremely difficult for us to take such proposals seriously. I would, therefore, like to conclude this speculation with a graph (Fig. 11) which shows the results of a rough attempt to estimate what the dollar value in today's market might be if such a thoroughgoing program of agrestal management and grassroots development in the northern New Mexico uplands, over a 25-year period, were to be carried out.

The left-hand ordinate represents the dollar value of the various 1960 "primary" regional revenues which I discussed earlier in this study. Excluding imported funds, manufacturing value-added, and mine output, the remaining revenues, amounting to about $40 million, may be ascribed to the use of biotic and environmental resources — forest products harvesting and processing, the recreational "industry," and agricultural production.

The right-hand ordinate, representing a mythical 1985, shows the dollar amount of these same revenues as they would stand if a program such as I have outlined above had been successfully carried out in each of the 60-odd watershed communities of the region. To arrive at these figures I have, of course, had to make some rather sweeping assumptions as to the recreational

91

"carrying power" of the wildlands, the probable yearly output of mixed conifer forests in semiarid climates under optimum sustained-yield management, and the manpower requirements of a highly intensive program of agrestal management. I have used such factual source material as was available, and I believe the order of magnitude of the cumulative total — about $400 million — to be reasonable. This represents a tenfold increase over the corresponding values for 1960.

The labor force necessary for such a combined "output" I estimate at about 50,000 — roughly a fivefold increase over the number engaged in the corresponding "primary" activities in 1960. The actual distribution of income is, as usual, very difficult to estimate but since, due to the nature of the process of capital formation, a minimum of debt-servicing would be involved and, since much of the capital installation would be either small-scale and privately owned, or cooperatively administered, it is reasonable to assume that the actual per capita income would approach the average, and would be about twice that of 1960. This rough calculation makes no allowance for the contributions of the subsistence sector of the regional economy, which would be much larger absolutely and somewhat larger, proportionately, than they were in 1960. Nor does it assign any value to the overall improvement in water yield, flood retardation, sediment control, and aquifer recharging, which could be of major benefit to the three principal drainage basins.

That social and economic benefits of this order of magnitude, contributing to both local and national well-being can, in principle, be achieved by a simple grassroots type of technical and organizational development in a region of this kind, and that the cultural tradition and the social morphology of the region favor such a development, seems to me highly significant. I believe I am justified in feeling that this "bioeconomic" approach to economic development offers the key to one of the most perplexing problems facing society today.

In sum, I suggest that this approach to regional development offers, in principle, a very remarkable potential for economic and social benefit. This benefit can be realized without large-scale subsidies or investments, and without the traumatic displacement of a deeply rooted culture. It can accrue to both local residents, the State, and the whole nation. It can be realized by reasonable and feasible programs conceived in harmony with both the

92

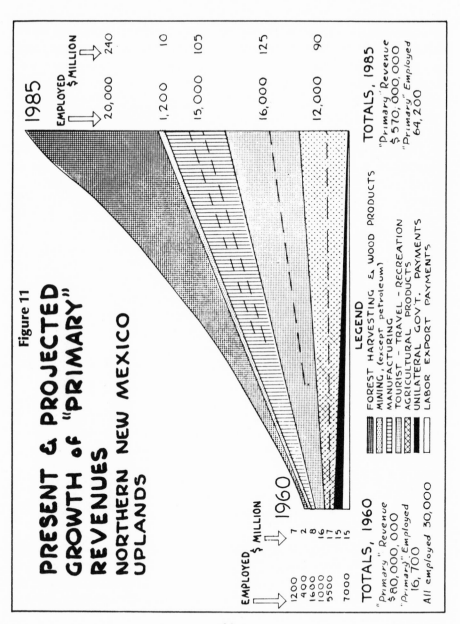

Figure 11

PRESENT & PROJECTED GROWTH of "PRIMARY" REVENUES
NORTHERN NEW MEXICO UPLANDS

1960

EMPLOYED $ MILLION

1200	7
400	2
1600	8
1000	16
5500	17
	15
7000	15

TOTALS, 1960
"Primary" Revenue
$ 80,000,000
"Primary" Employed
16,700
All employed 30,000

1985

EMPLOYED $ MILLION

20,000	240
1,200	10
15,000	105
16,000	125
12,000	90

TOTALS, 1985
"Primary" Revenue
$ 570,000,000
"Primary" Employed
64,200

LEGEND
FOREST HARVESTING & WOOD PRODUCTS
MINING, (except petroleum)
MANUFACTURING
TOURIST – TRAVEL – RECREATION
AGRICULTURAL PRODUCTS
UNILATERAL GOVT. PAYMENTS
LABOR EXPORT PAYMENTS

physical realities of the terrain and topography and the basic dynamics of the regional culture. I suggest it is worth at least as serious and intensive study as is now devoted to the alternative rationale of big-scale investment, monolithically administered projects. and giant public works.

PART FOUR
WHAT ARE
NATURAL RESOURCES?

PART FOUR

WHAT ARE NATURAL RESOURCES?

The Mercantilist Bias

In discussing the economic future of a region such as 'the uplands, a question invariably comes up: "But what resources do you have there? Uranium? Oil? Do you have workable deposits of coal, copper, gold? Can your wheat fields compete with Kansas or your forests with Oregon? What do you expect to base your economic development on?"

Such questions arise from an ingrained habit of thought dating from the 18th century mercantile revolution which views "natural resources" as only those minerals or vegetable products which can be extracted or produced in bulk and shipped en masse to satisfy the specialized needs of urban-industrial markets. It is upon such commodities — rubber, cotton, wool, tobacco, sugar, coffee, tin, copper, petroleum — that the classic colonial pattern of "economic development" has been built. This pattern has prevailed not only between nations — as in the 19th century world of European manufacturing states vis-a-vis tropical plantation dependencies — but *within* nations in the form of enclaved districts, tied to distant industrial and financial capitals, and devoted to monocultural "agribusiness" or to the mining of crude minerals.

Under this philosophy, and the investment and industrial practices arising from it, the typical "lagging" or "underdeveloped" region must languish in limbo unless the decision-makers of megalopolis can discover within it some "natural resource" occurring in sufficient quantity and accessibility to warrant extensive investment in its extraction and its export for competitive sale on the continental market. This single-minded view of the nature of economic resources has pock-marked the nation with enclaves of permanent depression — the coal counties of Appalachia, the cut-over lands of the upper Middle West, the eroded cotton and tobacco hinterlands of the Southeast. In these regions, an initial dominance of a monocultural cash crop has impeded the growth of a diversified economy and forced a specialized export-oriented one, which later collapsed — due to the exhaustion of the single natural resource on which it was based, to more efficient production elsewhere, or to obsolescence of the product.

"Natural Resources" in the Bioeconomic Context

The irony in all this is that a great many of these rural and provincial hinterlands and enclaves actually do possess a range of natural resources, defined in a broader and more basic sense, to generously fill the bulk of human needs. Here can usually be found sufficient arable land to raise most of the food needed by the community; timber and common minerals in sufficient abundance for buildings, equipment, and tools; an average variety of plant and animal life for meat, fiber, fuel, and textiles; various climatic and environmental amenities. Out of such taken-for-granted factors, an ingenious and intelligent people can fabricate most of the necessaries and many of the embellishments of a good society. Little matter that most of these commonplace resources cannot be barrelled or baled and shipped to Rotterdam, New York, or Istanbul for cash. Shaped by an appropriate technology, agriculture, and architecture; distributed by a reasonably efficient and equable system of trade and exchange, they can go far toward provisioning, housing, and equipping a thriving regional community.

This sort of ability to "live within one's means," in terms of the basic environmental resources of a reasonably well-endowed territory has been, of course, the norm for most human communities throughout most of history. It is probable that, despite the spectacular feats of high-energy technology and massive transport, a return to this norm— at a new and higher level of sophistication and scientific competence — offers the one bright hope for the many have-not, "underdeveloped," and proto-industrial regions of the globe. It is also possible that this sort of sociotechnical evolution will do much to correct the serious ecologic and environmental unbalances which overdependence on giant industry, supertransport, and the megalopolitan version of habitat, have generated.

In this book, I have argued that:

• Traditional communities of the New Mexico upland region have, in many ways, lived out and embodied this principle of ecologic adaptation, albeit in simple and basic terms.

• Through historical and geographical circumstances, this pattern of life and livelihood is still vital throughout much of this unique province within the United States, and its physical basis in the landscape has not yet been destroyed by the march of urban-industrial reorganization and "rationalization."

• This region, therefore, offers a very special opportunity for the understanding of an ecologically adapted way of life, and for the evolution of a "bioeconomic" society oriented towards a desirable and feasible future.

How, then, do the economic resources of the Hispanic Rockies shape up in the light of such principles? Let us attempt a brief inventory of a few elementary ones, along with some comments.

Arable and pastoral land — As explained elsewhere in this book, there is sufficient land in these categories to feed several times the present regional population at a high level of nutrition. But this goal requires intensive and diversified cultivation of high vitamin and protein crops and the raising, fattening, and processing of livestock *primarily for local and regional consumption.* Attempts to compete on the national market in the mercantilist tradition, either with bulk field crops or with the mass export of cattle on the hoof, will fall far short of realizing the full value of this basic resource to the community, and will perpetuate the second-class "colonial" status of the regional economy.

Timber — There are about 5,000 square miles of "commercial" timberlands in the uplands, but the rough and often inaccessible terrain, and

99

the variegated and pocketed stands, put this resource at a disadvantage in comparison with large uniform managed forests of the Pacific Coast, the Southeast, and elsewhere. Export of rough timber from the uplands brings relatively little employment and income to the regional community. But the yield is ample to supply the regional building industry, where availability and low cost are real economic assets, and where the indigenous architecture can adapt to the characteristics of the material. Small-scale localized industries carrying wood products to the most finished stages (residence, resort, recreational, and utilitarian structures; Southwestern furniture; moldings and trim; wood specialities, craft products, etc.) would yield far more regional income and employment than the present export of logs or rough lumber. They would also provide high-value commodities for outregion exchange.

As an almost incidental byproduct to this general process of wood harvesting and processing, the fuel needs of the region could be met at low cost, thus reducing still further the need for "foreign exchange," and for plundering the non-renewable fossil-fuel bank of the nation.

Earth — The justly famous technique of *adobe*-and-*viga* construction converts this virtually free material into a major economic asset — low-cost housing available to all. In the hands of perceptive architects, this material can also be worked up into specialized structures of considerable sophistication, beauty, and functionality. The currently fashionable tendency to import pre-fab structures and manufactured building materials, under the pressures of metropolitan costs and urgencies, is a symptom of malfunction and unbalance in this traditionally well-adapted sector of the regional economy.

Hides and wool — Wool from the many thousands of sheep grazed in northern New Mexico is sold "in the grease" at thirty cents a pound or less to jobbers for export to the mills of New England and the Middle West. Under this arrangement, a thousand sheep grazing many sections of land will

100

support one family and a few sheepherders. A localized spinning and textile industry would increase many times the value of this basic raw material, both for local needs and for high-value export. Similarly, hides from cattle slaughtered in the region are picked up by itinerant traders for a dollar or so each, to be shipped to St. Louis for tanning. Processed into good leather, these same hides sell for a dollar a square foot. Worked up into specialty leather goods, they may command a dollar a square inch. The inference is obvious.

Environmental amenities — These intangibles generate very real economic assets for the region, although difficult to evaluate in conventional mercantilist terms. Most fundamental, perhaps, the very dispersion and decentralization of the fertile valleys, forests, and waters here make possible and logical communities within which, or close at hand, may be found many of the requirements for material survival and for the good life. This alone reduces the need for elaborate transit and travel patterns which are costing our metropolitan and suburban world so heavily.

Next to this factor, the siting of villages and "bioeconomic communities" in the verdant valleys amidst the panoramas of the southern Rockies provide, at no cost, advantages which in less fortunate parts of the country must be paid for in cash, in the forms of parks, expensive subdivisions, vacation trips, etc. These amenities may be capitalized on and may yield essential money values to the regional community, through the provision of recreation and resort facilities for visitors from afar.

But this type of resources-exploitation must be entered upon with the greatest care and moderation. Massive money (whether public or private) invested in enormous dams and scenic freeways, in recreation complexes and retirement cities, can monopolize the best sites and waters for non-productive use, can — like any other monocultural industry — destroy a sound and diversified regional economy, and can, by importing all the problems of a high-energy, high-consumption megalopolitan economy, disrupt the natural balance of the landscape. Resort and recreational facilities should be small-scale and dispersed, and should be integrated with the economic and civic life of the organic communities. Handled in this fashion, the intangible environmental amenities of this region can round out the basis for healthy and enduring growth.

Seen in this perspective, the question is not whether northern New Mexico is well enough endowed with "natural resources" to justify economic development in the traditional sense. The question, rather, is whether we can modify our institutions and values to allow the people of this regional community to make effective use of the wide range of basic life-supporting factors which nature offers.

Assuredly, if we can achieve this sort of adaptation, the lessons learned will have very wide application.

ECOLOGIC ADAPTATION AND THE URBAN FUNCTION

PART FIVE

ECOLOGIC ADAPTATION AND THE URBAN FUNCTION

Since unavoidably the ecologic challenge looms to most of us today as a crisis of the urban environment, the relevance of the preceding arguments to the overriding problem of urban development in New Mexico must be an essential test of their validity.

In advocating a process of socioeconomic adaptation to the biologic and ecologic capabilities of the region, are we by the same token advocating an abandonment of the indispensible civilizing and horizon-enlarging function of city and town, a regression to an artificial and narrow parochialism and rusticity as the price of survival?

The intent is otherwise. Evidence has been presented that conditions are favorable within this region for the incubation of a future-oriented pattern of dispersed urbanism in which many of the amenities, technical refinements, and diversified and complementary activities of a mature society may be cultivated in humanly scaled communities functioning close to the land and its life cycles.

Let us recapitulate the narrative leading to such conditions.

We begin our observations with the interesting coincidence that the great triangular peninsula of mountainous highlands formed by the southernmost Rockies thrusting across the Colorado border into New Mexico, covers an area roughly equal to Switzerland. While this uplands province is defined by no official boundary, and has no existence as a chartered political entity, it is actually one of the most distinctive and homogeneous regions within the United States. Outside of a few centers

105

where such national-establishment-servicing activities as tourism, retirement servicing, and research in nuclear technology have evolved mainly within the past generation, it is overwhelmingly Hispanic in population and cultural heritage. It is furthermore strongly folk- and village-oriented in its demography and its settlement pattern. In its commitment to subsistence agriculture, pastoral husbandry, and the livelihoods of woodlands and forest, it provides a social milieu in which many of the values and traditions of late-medieval Galicia, Asturias, or Estremadura (tinctured with Ute or Tewa influences in the new world) have been operative well into the 20th century.

The life-style, architecture, and cultural atmosphere resulting from this combination of factors has until recently set apart the region as unique in the United States. Santa Fé, its miniature provincial capital, has seemed almost a legendary antique outpost to travelers from the east, while the world of remote mesas and peaks, of quiet streamside pueblos or mountain hamlets to the north has beckoned to generations of artists, writers, and refugees from the tensions of metropolitan America.

It is no news that this overstylized picture has been changing, and with increasing rapidity, since the 1950s at least. The expanding continental network of transport, commerce, and finance has permeated more and more thoroughly the social and economic life of the Hispanic enclave. The sophisticated goods, services, and techniques of urban-industrial civilization have increasingly displaced the agrarian and folk modes, and with them have come the rising costs and taxes of a monetized economy. A substantial proportion of the local population has adapted to, facilitated, and sometimes profited by these changes. Additionally, streams of settlers from the rest of the nation have poured into the few cities of New Mexico which could act as foci for the newer commercial, fiscal, and administrative operations, and thus offer employment opportunities. These cities have accordingly boomed with new construction, new industries and services, new payrolls, new subdivisions.

But inevitably they have also begun to experience the stereotyped problems and dislocations of unbalanced metropolitan growth — traffic overload, suburban sprawl, environmental deterioration, water and energy shortage, pollution, financial embarrassment, class discrimination. And at the same time the long-settled rural and village hinterlands have been experiencing the corresponding stereotype of economic stagnation,

106

depopulation, outmigration of youth, community decay, and deterioration of farms and villages.

Our nation as a whole has lived with this syndrome for a century or more now: Progress at a Price — the skyscrapers of a Chicago, a Denver, or a Phoenix paired against whole provinces of moribund towns and minor cities in Appalachia, the Southeast, the Great Plains; a vast freeway network achieved at shattering cost to natural ecology and human communities; enormous GNP in mobility, gadgetry, and expertise maintained through reckless overdrafts against natural resources, quality of environment, and international goodwill.

Is this polarization of progress really inevitable — a law of nature? Here in New Mexico the process is relatively new. And here also the margin for absorbing its negative aspects is slimmer. The reasons for this have long been known amongst conservationists and are beginning to be publicly discussed with the rise of the ecology and environment crusade. Erodable terrain, fragile vegetative cover, semi-arid climate, sparse water supply — all combine to underscore the idea that man's occupancy and use of this land be handled with particular caution and understanding. In this perspective the possibility of metrocenters on the current pattern, with their insatiable appetites for water and the combustion of fuels, their vast expanses of asphalt accelerating storm runoff and valley flooding, their unmanageable outputs of wastes, looms as a permanent catastrophe for New Mexico. The suburbs and satellites built to satisfy the recreational and retirement needs of such urban aggregations enlarge enormously the scope of their ecologic destructiveness through wholesale bulldozing of access roads and building sites and through depletion of aquifers for unproductively used water. The massive systems of freeways necessary to provide for the commuting habits of their populations further disrupt the hydrology and ecology of the landscape, and lower the productivity of the fertile valleys through which they pass. The great dams built to irrigate and (supposedly) protect from floods the industrial farms set up for their provisioning, unbalance the regimens of entire river basins, and waste water unconscionably through evaporation, siltation, and the encouragement of weed phreatophytes. And all these technological requirements combine to monopolize available social energy and skill in such a way as to block its effective employment in conservative and regenerative care of the land and the living community we

107

share it with.

Lest we think this inventory of the side effects of progress is exaggerated, we must bear in mind that we are only at the beginning of the cycle of development in New Mexico; that knowledgeable officials predict a quadrupling or quintupling of Santa Fé's population within a matter of 25 years; that utility engineers have suggested that its water requirements by 1995 can be realistically met only by "drying up" the irrigated farmlands of the upper Rio Grande Basin; that shrewd real estate men talk confidently of a 100-mile long highway city from Albuquerque to Espanola and beyond in a decade or so: that a quarter of a million acres of chapparal lands in the northern region have currently been purchased and platted for suburban housing projects and the area increases each year.

Certainly we must provide for a healthy growth in population in balance with the carrying power of this land. Certainly we must draw heavily upon science to improve the skill with which we work with our animate and inanimate resources. Certainly we must eliminate enclaves of human impoverishment and disadvantage. Certainly to denounce science and technology, to call for "undevelopment" and a turn to the primitive or to karmic non-attachment is to retreat into fantasy. But equally certainly, to accept the formulas of economic, industrial, and urban development as we have known them since before the Civil War is, in the present context, equally to fantasize and, in the long run, more dangerously.

Can we, in fact, conceive of an alternative pattern of urban settlement and technologic improvement which will not, like the proverbial successful operation in the course of which the patient dies, destroy New Mexico in the process of solving its economic problems?

The answer may lie, quite simply, in an extension and refinement of the principles which have guided the colonization and occupancy of the New Mexico Rocky Mountains over the past several centuries. For here we have an inescapable "logic of the land" and of permanent human habitation — a pattern of ecologically adapted communities ·strategically planted in the numerous fertile valleys of the region, and drawing their livelihood mainly from the irrigated bottom lands, the uplands meadows, the pastoral woodlands, and the forests surrounding them.

Because this way of life (along with the terrain on which it is based) is not amenable to the large-scale, centralized, and mechanized functions on

108

which our metropolitan-dominated economy is based; because it still bears the stamp of the earlier handicraft era in which it evolved; and because it has not thrived under an alien system of laws, land controls, and social institutions, over the past hundred years, it has become the habit to dismiss it as archaic, inefficient, and outmoded.

If we can overcome this prejudice and look at this great region both with an unbiased eye for the cares and labors of centuries embodied in it, and with insights derived from the current renaissance in the ecologic and environmental sciences, we may paradoxically discover here a truer shape for the future than our current conventional wisdom conceives. For does the opportunity for fruitful human survival in this part of the world lie in a senseless mechanical multiplication of population in two or three stereotyped consumer-cities located at transport hubs, with a vast expanse of prefabricated amusement and retirement suburbs and satellites tied to them? Or might it more hopefully lie in a constellation of organically formed communities, sited throughout the fertile valleys of this favored uplands province, and drawing their sustenance from skilled and scientific use of the biotic resources around them? Should we be thinking, to be specific, not in conventional city planning terms of a Santa Fé - Los Alamos - Española metropolis of endlessly proliferating freeways, traffic interchanges, supermarket plazas, and motel convention centers, but of an uplands province of dispersed and decentralized smaller towns and new-era villages?

With economies built around intensive high-value agriculture on the irrigated valley lands, scientific silviculture, and wood products technology in the forests, small-scale skill intensive industries, and tourist facilities in the villages, there is no physical reason why such productive communities should not house, provision, and provide life's amenities to a regional population of at least half a million. This could be done with agricultural techniques no more sophisticated than have been practiced in the advanced European countries for the past fifty years or more. (Switzerland, for example, with arable lands probably no more than 5 times greater in area than the irrigable bottomlands of northern New Mexico, and with a climate so rigorous that crops will generally not grow above 4,000 feet, was a generation ago feeding two and a half million citizens from its small mountain farms, and still producing millions of francs worth of high quality dairy products for export.) And paradoxically, with such an intensive agronomy, the soils and forests of the region could be better cared for from the conservationist point of view than they are at present. It is a truism that the higher the value and intensity of agricultural or silvicultural land use, the more it is possible to devote effort and manpower to its proper maintenance and ecologic management.

From the hydrologic point of view, such a pattern of dispersed "micro-urban" development would make far more efficient use of available water than the current rationale of massive downstream urban expansion and monocultural plantations. Rainfall and snowmelt would be largely utilized near their source, with the minimum of evaporative and transport losses (which amount to at least 50% for the typical great mainstream dam and channel installations). Multi-million dollar engineering works would, in fact, be unnecessary and obsolete in this context, and the huge public funds now devoted to them could be spent for better purposes. True multiple use of the precious water would be automatically achieved because of the inherent nature of ecologically balanced communities, in which agriculture, industrial, and domestic use would be part of a close-coupled symbiotic arrangement. And finally, due to the more effective soil and vegetative management throughout the region, subsoil percolation could be greatly improved, underground water storage maximized, and the permanent flow of downstream portions of the regional rivers stabilized.

In terms of energetics and pollution concern, such a predominantly biotically based regional society could have a far gentler impact on the environment than the alternative urban-industrial metro-complex monopolizing the same natural resources. Due to the relative self-containment of the region in such essentials as food production and building technology, far less demand for heavy transportation and heavy industrial processing would be generated. Close and efficient recycling of organic wastes would be both feasible and economically justified. The staggering burden of disposal inherent in a centralized mass-distribution containerized logistic system would be eliminated. The use of solar and wind energy — both suited to the climate and to decentralized operations — could be deliberately and justifiably fostered. The skilled employment of simple ready-to-hand raw materials (timber, earth, rock) for most domestic and institutional construction, could further reduce the regional dependence on the energy- and materials-consuming continental urban-industrial system.

110

Finally, from the social and human point of view, such a regional economy could evolve naturally and satisfyingly from the customary life and livelihood modes here established. The physical matrix of village and pueblo closely associated with irrigated farmlands already embodies the essential principles of spatial arrangement, land-use, and basic logistics. The tradition of careful husbandry; of long-term involvement with the affairs of fields, meadows and forests; of family and community management of *acequia* systems, grazing arrangements, crop gathering and storage lead naturally into the evolution of more sophisticated bio-urban communities, given any sort of favorable institutional environment.

And such an evolutionary process, it may in conclusion be pointed out, offers by far the best hope of resolving in a constructive way, the sterile ethnic and racial confrontations which must automatically arise as the bulldozer of rigidly conceived megatechnic "progress" continues to invade New Mexico.

One must obviously postscript such utopian speculations with a dim view of our present collective ability to engineer this sort of an urban revolution in the shape of New Mexico's socio-economic future. Rather sweeping changes in many sectors of long-fixed public and quasi-public policy — in education, in finance, in public lands and waters control, in road-building rationale, in local and municipal government, in technical and scientific research goals — would be necessary. And all these changes would have to be mutually compatible and mutually reinforcing. Some of them may be foreshadowed in such social expressions as environment and ecology concern, in minority rights campaigns, in youth secessionary tendencies, in educational reform demands. But these expressions are often fragmentary and even mutually contradictory, and so far have little effect on the basic formative processes of the social organism. Yet the need for a life-affirming alternative to the excessively mechanistic version of progress which dominates us is urgent and intensely practical; and one may still insist that the circumstances for realizing it are more favorable in New Mexico than elsewhere in the nation.

111

ADDENDUM

ADDENDUM

The following resolution was presented to the 20th International Design Conference at Aspen, Colorado, devoted to the question of "Environment by Design," and was endorsed by acclamation in full session on June 19, 1970. It is reprinted here as a succinct summing up of the approach set forth in the main body of this book.

RESOLVED THAT:

A substantial portion of our social effort must be directed toward the revitalization of the entire range of smaller rural and provincial communities, this renewal to be based on skilled, scientific, and conservative use and management of local biotic and other flow resources, rather than on large-scale machine- and energy-intensive industries and heavy transport. This end to be furthered by:

1. Research on technology appropriate to communities of this type such as construction with abundant and cost-free indigenous materials; intensive agriculture, food production, and storage; utilization of solar, wind, and other non-polluting and non-consumptive energy sources; close recycling of waste products for maintenance of organic fertility; miscellaneous essential small-scale industries using local resources.

2. Research on planning, micro-urban design, circulation and communication design, land-use management, and similar techniques capable of enhancing the logistic and functional effectiveness of such communities as well as their esthetic and cultural vitality.

3. Encouraging education and training practices which permit the fullest application of knowledge and skills appropriate to such regional and indigenous needs and functions.

4. Revision of public policies in such fields as credit, land taxation and tenure, and corporate and cooperative franchises so as to maximize opportunities for the establishment of community-serving productive enterprises.

5. Revising the mandates of major land and water custodial agencies to emphasize management of such resources for ecologically grounded regional

communities rather than exclusively for the satisfaction of urban and metropolitan needs.

6. Placing more emphasis in highway policy on tertiary low-cost road systems for internal regional circulation and less on the high-speed intermetropolitan systems. Careful design of highways should minimize disruption of communities, fertile valleys, and ecological balance.

7. Encouragement of forms of local and regional government with greater competency and responsibility to reinforce such policies intelligently.

THE AUTHOR

Photograph by James B. DeKorne

A 1930-vintage dropout from Cornell University (where he studied engineering and architecture), Peter van Dresser describes himself as having spent most of his adult life laboring on the groundwork of a personal economy outside the urban-industrial complex: first aboard the 32-foot ketch which was his home for several years on the Atlantic seaboard; next in south Florida on the fringes of the Everglades; next in the Delaware Valley; and for the last two decades in a mountain village of the New Mexican Rockies. Mr. van Dresser supports himself in what he describes as a "relatively non-exploitive way" by free-lance writing, occasional professional employment in city and regional planning, economic and technical research and architecture, and by subsistence livelihoods in homestead building, agriculture, and small enterprise.

In the mid-1930s, while living in New York City, he participated in some of the earliest non-military research on rocket propulsion, as a member of the American Rocket Society's Experiment Committee which developed the first successful regeneratively cooled liquid propellant rocket motor in America (in 1937), and as editor of the Society's journal, *Astronautics*. His papers from that period are in the Smithsonian's astronautics collection.

He also has had a long-term interest in simple utilization of solar and wind energy, having built solar domestic water heaters in Florida and a sun-tempered adobe house in Santa Fe in 1958. He and his wife Florence maintain their "ecologic niche" in a small country inn and restaurant in their adopted village, where they grow much of their own food and are guided as much as possible by the concept of ecologic adaptation discussed in this book. The appeal of their life-style to their grandchildren, they feel, is one of their major rewards.